LOVE OF GOLD

LOVE
OF
GOLD

EMILY HAHN

LIPPINCOTT & CROWELL, PUBLISHERS

NEW YORK

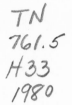

TN
761.5
H33
1980

To
Muriel Ripperger Hanson,
good friend

Grateful acknowledgment is made for permission to reprint:

Excerpts from "Brazilian Gold and British Traders in the First Half of the Eighteenth Century" by C. R. Boxer, which first appeared in the August 1969 issue of *Hispanic American Historical Review.* Copyright 1969 by Duke University Press. Reprinted by permission.

Excerpts from *The Golden Age of Brazil* by C. R. Boxer. Copyright 1962 by The Regents of the University of California. Reprinted by permission of the University of California Press.

FIRST EDITION

Designer: Vikki Sheatsley

Library of Congress Cataloging in Publication Data

Hahn, Emily, 1905–
  Love of gold.
  Bibliography: p. 173
  Includes index.
  1. Gold. I. Title.
TN761.5.H33 1980   669'.22   80–7877
ISBN 0–690–01832–0

80 81 82 83 84 10 9 8 7 6 5 4 3 2 1

CONTENTS

Gold! gold! gold! gold!
Bright and yellow, hard and cold,
Molten, graven, hammer'd and roll'd;
Heavy to get, and light to hold;
Hoarded, barter'd, bought, and sold,
Stolen, borrow'd, squander'd, doled:
Spurn'd by the young, but hugg'd by the old
To the very verge of the churchyard mould;
Price of many a crime untold;
Gold! gold! gold! gold:
Good or bad a thousand-fold!
How widely its agencies vary—
To save—to ruin—to curse—to bless—
As even its minted coins express,
Now stamp'd with the image of Good Queen Bess,
And now of a Bloody Mary!

—Thomas Hood,
"Miss Kilmansegg and Her Precious Leg.
A Golden Legend"

1

ANCIENT TREASURE

GOLD. . . . Precious non-rusting metal sometimes used in
the Middle Ages in thin leaves for wrapping some pastes
and certain roast birds (gold is still used for this purpose in
the Far East).

—Larousse Gastronomique

The radio announcer said, "In London this morning gold was
up again; it hit six hundred and eighty. Two points lower in
Zurich. . . ."

I waited to see if the dollar had sunk. Sometimes it does. In the
olden days (like a year ago) we knew that the dollar plays a game
of seesaw with gold; it is a bad sign for American currency when
the price of gold goes up and a good sign when it sinks. That is
what we used to think, but as I later found out, it's not necessarily
true.

Six hundred and eighty! It seemed to me that I heard, all over
New York, the sound of strongboxes being pulled out and the
chink of metal as housewives counted out their broken bits of
silver and gold bracelets. I imagined people hovering over the
family silver, asking themselves if it was sterling or plate. Six
hundred and eighty. . . .

Do I really understand all this? Barely. I only know that people
want to keep their money safe, so when their currency gets
shaky, when they can buy less—especially in markets abroad—
than they could yesterday, they hurry to buy gold rather than
more currency. (That is to say, they buy gold when they are
permitted to do so, which is not always.) Think of French peas-
ants and their stockings full of money which they won't trust to
banks: They would change it into gold if they could, and often
they can and do. Think of Indian women and their heavy gold

1

necklaces, often representing their dowries. The Greeks, too, and the Turks—they all do it. Gold is preferred over money every time. Sometimes it's the same thing as money, but more often, as in times of war, it most certainly is not.

Since gold is not necessarily money, my fondness for it is no mere miserliness, I tell myself reassuringly. Gold fascinates me. I love it, and it is reassuring to read the opinion of an expert, Pierre Vilar, who, in *A History of Gold and Money, 1450–1920,* wrote, "My theme is gold and gold is quite different from money. Gold is a mineral substance. It has its own technology, its own geography and its own economics as an artistic and industrial substance."

So there it is: I am no mere miser. Gold simply pleases me; don't ask me why. Whenever I travel to a new country I like to buy something, however small, made of it. Like many other people I have my own firm ideas of what it should be like in color: not too pale, if possible somewhat ruddy, and because this is such a purely personal matter, it does not shake me to be told that the color of gold depends on what kind of alloy is used in it. (I have been shy about buying even the smallest golden article when it is almost pure, ever since I brought back a ring of nearly twenty-four-carat gold and gave it to my small daughter. When, a few days later, I asked where it had gone, she said, "Oh, that ring was no good. It bent up and broke, so I threw it away.")

I have a chain made of Chinese gold and golden earrings from Turkey which I never wear. I just like to know they are there, safe in the bank. Oh, well, maybe I *am* a miser.

Not only do I like gold, I trust it, and in this I am not, of course, unique. Many of us after two full-blown wars feel the same way. If I were given my choice of portable valuables to take with me in flight, I would undoubtedly grab what I could of gold, even though in quantity it tends to be heavy. Again, I am not unique; far from it. The word *instinct* is not useful these days, its meaning having been leached out by over-definition, so I cannot say that human beings have an instinct for loving and saving gold, but if I were writing carelessly I might say something of the sort—and it would not be universally true. Though it is hard for me to believe, there do exist people who don't care for the metal or value it as much as a bowerbird cares for pretty pieces of blue glass. You have to look for such people, in out-of-the-way places of the earth, but they can be found, or could be found, in the South Sea Islands (more about them later).

Conditions change people's opinions on gold, too. During the last world war, soldiers in occupied areas where people were starving discovered that they could swap soap, chocolate, and rations for practically any service they desired, while gold would not have taken them far. A man I was acquainted with, when he was in Japan just after the surrender of that country to the Allies, parlayed a carton of cigarettes into a fortune—with which, for all I know, he invested heavily in gold. Remember King Midas, who turned everything he touched into gold, then discovered to his grief that he couldn't eat or drink it and became very unhappy before he was able to change matters. Midas with his golden touch is a legend, but a significant one, showing that the ancient Greeks had noted the same phenomenon I am discussing.

We humans are odd and exasperating, as economists are well aware. Looked at from a distance, nothing could be less sensible than our fixation on a soft, malleable, easily eroded mineral as a standard of value, but these things are not deliberately developed or reasonably evolved. To be sure, there are certain arguments to the credit of gold as a symbol of money. It is the best example offered by our planet of a "noble" metal, a substance that does not rust. (That is why all the gold that has ever been mined still exists. It has probably been melted down ten times over to make new ingots, watch chains, rings, idols, whatever. Some of the gold in your wedding ring or your earrings might well have come from Egypt or Babylon or the Indian desert.) Platinum, gold's closest rival in nobility, never really took off or won the affection of the public. It is true that platinum hasn't as long a pedigree: Nobody knew about it until comparatively recently, but even though we now know that it is even rarer than gold and less liable to oxidation, few pretty ladies are likely to go overboard for platinum jewelry, and it has never been adopted for coinage. For one thing, it looks too much like silver, so that only the initiate can be sure that platinum jewels did indeed cost a tremendous lot. The agitated fear of a dentist I knew, soon after platinum came on the scene and was briefly popular, that its adoption by craftsmen for frivolous purposes would endanger the supply urgently needed by people in his profession, was, happily, unjustified. It is true that platinum, like gold, is very useful. It, too, does not tarnish; it, too, is malleable; it, too, is valuable—you can get a lot of money for platinum. It just hasn't any appeal. Even if it had been more generally known in ancient days it wouldn't have taken hold. You seldom, if ever, find platinum votive offerings in religious haunts, or platinum-edged pages in precious books, or platinum-trimmed bibelots made by Fabergé and his apprentices.

Now gold most decidedly does have appeal. I learned this a long time ago. Stopping for the night in a small town in East Africa, I had a drink or two with the Greek proprietor, of the general store as well as the humble lodging house. After the second drink, becoming confidential, he told me that he had made his fortune, or at any rate was about to, out of a secret supply of treasure he had found on his bit of land. After the third drink he went and brought out a sample of the treasure, putting it down proudly before me on the bare, beer-spotted table. It was a handful of mineral samples, and I examined a few of the pieces. They were a pale brassy color and were roughly regular in shape, like warped cubes, with striations on their flat planes.

"That's gold!" said the Greek.

I shook my head. "I don't think so. I think it's iron pyrites," I replied, "or maybe lead." After all, I studied mineralogy at college.

"It's *gold*," said the Greek.

"No," I said. I was an unpleasantly opinionated young woman in those days.

He slammed the table with his fist, shouting, "It's *go-old!*" and something in the mad glitter of those eyes behind the spectacles taught me caution, however belatedly.

"If you say so," I muttered, and went to bed soon afterward. He did not see me off in the morning. Never mind; somewhere, I hope, he is still dreaming dreams over his little hoard.

It is tempting to say that all this romantic love for a soft yellow metal (though I resent the word *yellow* in this connotation; gold is gold, like no other color in the world) comes out of our childhood and the fairy stories we heard then. Fairy stories reflect the adult cultures of yesterday, and obviously something in us still responds to the glitter and beauty of gold, as to a Christmas tree's tinsel. Nor is it true that we think of it as money, although we find it useful for making coins; but long before we selected gold as a good mineral for coinage we were using other substances for small change—lead, copper, and shells. A prize example often trotted out by me is the population of the island of Yap in the Pacific, where the natives used to traffic with millstones, or at least objects very like millstones in widely varying sizes. The larger such a stone was, the more it was worth, though we cannot tell why. Medium-sized ones could at least be carried around by means of poles stuck through the hole in the middle—incidentally, that hole was always square—whereas a prize big stone stayed wherever it was, safe from theft because of its weight but decidedly in the way. Big ones were also well-known in themselves. Everyone on Yap knew the pedigree and ownership of every single monster stone, and in a small community this had its advantages.

Not just any old stone would do. These particular treasures are composed of aragonite, a mineral that does not occur naturally on Yap but must be quarried on either Guam or Pelew, neighboring islands where aragonite has no monetary value save that quarrying rights have to be paid for by the inhabitants of Yap. In former days when the stones were the only currency available to —or, rather, accepted by—Yappites, they were chopped out of their native rock and brought over by boat, a hazardous proceeding considering the weight of the load and the fragility of the craft. Paul Einzig has pointed out in his book *Primitive Money* that the beauty of this millstone currency is that it has absolutely no nonmonetary use and owes its value to three circumstances: its scarcity on Yap, its immense production costs (what with having to pay the workers who extract and transport it, as well as the kings who own the quarries), and the chances of the carriers capsizing. For example, on one expedition to Guam to fetch some stones, only one boat out of twenty ever returned. Fortunately, in the old days such capsizings didn't matter. If a giant millstone being carried from one island to another happened to be lost in the water and everyone knew just where it was, the owner continued to be the owner in the eyes of his world. As Einzig wrote, "A large stone which fell into the ocean was considered to form part of the possessions of the heirs of those who owned it." An heir could actually buy things with his submerged stone. "To Mr. Smith," one imagines the bill of sale, "in payment for his field, the stone at the bottom of the strait off Guam, at such-and-such longitude, such-and-such latitude. . . ."

While it may seem very strange to us, the Yap islanders have neighbors whose systems of money—in the old days more than now—appear equally inefficient, though they do not lead to quite as many difficulties as the millstones. The Samoans, for example, used to trade with fine handmade mats. The Fijians preferred whale's teeth. Nowadays all of them, Yappites, Samoans, and Fijians, are willing to accept our kind of money as specie, but millstones, mats, and whale's teeth are still not completely rejected.

None of this may seem particularly apposite to the subject of gold, but there is a connection of sorts. We all, as modern Americans say, have our hang-ups, and in the last analysis gold is as much a hang-up as whale's teeth and no more . . . or is it? I don't think it is; I think there is more, intrinsically, to gold. If there proves to be life on another planet and if we ever manage to get into communication with it, I shall be very surprised if we find that the inhabitants of that far-off country have not discovered gold and do not prize it highly—always according to their strange foreign customs, of course. Like the people of various South American civilizations they may do without money and coinage, but like those same South Americans they will use the mineral in other ways, perhaps forming vessels of it, or idols, or even—as did the Caribs encountered by Christopher Columbus on his first voyage—fishhooks. Or, if those other-planet beings are so constituted that they have no use for vessels or fishhooks, they will have figured out some other way to employ gold. Perhaps, like me, they simply like to look at it.

Although we didn't always use golden money, we have used gold itself for thousands of years. Golden coins, a comparatively modern invention, are perhaps on their way out. This is a fact hard to grasp because we are conditioned to think of gold—no, to *feel* it—as the ultimate in value. "Good as gold," we say. "Pure gold," George III's queen, Charlotte, said of Fanny Burney to express her appreciation of her lady-in-waiting's qualities of loyalty and patience. When we speak of happiness in life we may refer to its golden hours, if not various golden ages. Why were the Egyptian pharaohs and their loved ones wrapped and lapped in golden coverings? Partly to preserve the mummies and partly to honor them, so that the dead nobles would be properly garbed when they met their ancestors in the afterworld. When one values gold in this way, money might well take a secondary position, as it often does among the rich and powerful. So the top Egyptians filled their tombs with gold—and incidentally killed innumerable slaves to get more of it from their mines. Today, it is hardly necessary to remind anyone in the United States, Britain, or France of Tutenkhamon, the boy king of Egypt, and the astonishingly fresh, untarnished color of his grave treasures. We all know that his tomb contained only a small part of what went into the ground in royal and noble tombs in his country, though most of them were ransacked before we of the modern world could find them and do our own ransacking. Yet in all this display, this lavish use of the metal, there was never a golden coin.

The man credited with inventing gold coins lived a long time ago by our standards, though not as long ago as Tutenkhamon. He was Alyattes, king of Lydia in the early sixth century B.C., and father of Croesus, who was king of Lydia in his turn—Croesus, who owned so much gold that we still call our rich men after him. But it was his father, Alyattes, who thought of using the precious metal for money, no doubt because he too had plenty of it. The coin that he designed and had executed was not like the other money, of baser metal, then in circulation. There were important differences quite apart from the constitution of the metal used. Where the other money was roughly rectangular in shape, not unlike the so-called pieces of eight minted and used by Europeans in the seventeenth and eighteenth centuries, Alyattes's golden coin was round, or circular. And speaking strictly, it was not made of pure gold but of the alloy of gold and silver then called *electrum,* which occurred naturally in large quantities in placer, or alluvial, deposits in the rivers of Lydia. Moreover, the coin was stamped with a distinctive picture representing the head of a roaring lion. At least one specimen of this money has survived, which is how we know what it looked like. The roundish shape is probably less regular now than it was when the coin

first came out of the mint, because people through whose hands
it passed pinched off little bits of electrum before handing it on.
In later centuries attempts were made to stop this practice by
milling the edges of valuable coins, and milling is still done even
when coins are not made of such valuable stuff. We would find
an unmilled coin very strange and unfinished in appearance.
Alyattes's lion looks rather like a piece of gold that was thrown
down to cool after melting and then stamped.

But let us go back thousands of years to Egyptian gold, which
was used before money was ever thought of. It was wealth, yes;
power, yes; but not money. Possibly five thousand years ago,
certainly three thousand, the pharaohs and priests of Egypt were
using the sacred metal to make objects for their gods and their
divine selves. They were able to do this because they had access
to so much of it, not only as gold dust in placer mining but in
place, as veins in hard rock. Though mining methods today are
not as brutal as they were in those times of slavery, there is not
much difference in the underlying principle: Crush the auriferous mother rock and extract the gold. Some of the artifacts found
in Egyptian burials prove that goldsmiths all those thousands of
years ago were fantastically accomplished in their techniques for
working the mineral. Not only did they learn in the earliest days
that they could beat it out into thin sheets, persuade it to meld
together under blows or over fire, and draw it out into wire
which could be twisted into patterns, they also learned how to do
repoussé work—that is, to hammer shapes into it from the wrong
side, so that the gold was raised into the pattern they wanted.
They developed the difficult trick of granulating gold, so that a
myriad of tiny grains or globules could be scattered over a golden
background in formal patterns and fused there. And anyone who
has studied Egyptian jewelry knows how cunningly the goldsmiths adapted the art of enameling to their material. They also
understood very well how to set precious or semiprecious stones
into gold.

They early learned from nature and, later, through laboratory
experiments how to alloy other metals with gold. They found that
they could make electrum themselves, producing a very beautiful, greenish-colored white gold. Of course it was not as malleable
as pure gold—few alloys are—but it was useful as well as beauti-

ful. In other combinations, they learned that a little copper gave gold a ruddy tinge, and iron made it dark. The goldsmith used these various alloys deliberately, so that the contrasts would spell out a pattern, as, indeed, goldsmiths still do. These ancient artists left very little in their field for us to discover.

The traveler and historian Herodotus, who visited Tyre in Egypt during the fifth century B.C., was much impressed by the gold he saw on all sides. He took pains while there to look at a temple of Hercules because he had heard that it was very highly venerated; he found it richly adorned with many offerings, including a pillar of solid gold. Moving on to Papremus, he viewed a god's image in a small wooden shrine that was covered with golden plates; there seemed no shortage of the precious metal anywhere in Egypt. Herodotus also wrote of an Egyptian prince, a son of Cheops, who, when his only child died, determined to do her honor in an unusual way. A hollow wooden cow was constructed in the kneeling position, according to his design, and coated with gold. Then the princess's body was laid in it as in a coffin. The cow and its burden were never buried but left on view in the royal palace at Sais, where Herodotus himself saw it. Most of the cow, he reported, was shrouded in a scarlet blanket, but he saw the head and neck and could testify that it was very thickly plated with gold, with a golden sun placed between the horns. Egyptian gold plating *was* very thick.

It was an Egyptian king, Amasis, who gave rise to another story told by Herodotus about gold. Amasis was not ruler by means of the customary route: He had not inherited his rank. Some of the people complained that they were being ruled by a commoner, a fact of which the king was aware. Among the treasures of the palace was a golden footpan which he sometimes used when guests banqueted with him and wanted to wash their feet, as was the custom in those days. Amasis ordered this pan broken and melted down. Then with the gold he had an image made of one of the Egyptian gods and set it up in a public place. The people came in numbers to worship the new image. Amasis waited until the god had collected a large crowd and then told them what he had done.

"Many of you have washed your feet in this gold," he added,

"just as I have. You put your feet into the dirty basin and washed off the dirt. Yet today you are bowing down to an image made of the same gold and do it reverence. It is the same with your attitude to me. I used to be merely a private person, but I have become your king, so you should honor and reverence me. Think about it."

The people saw the point and never again sneered at the king's humble origins. At least that is Herodotus's story.

The Nubian mines owned by the Egyptians must also have been the source of some, at least, of the gold used at Ur of the Chaldees. There is no sign of gold mining or natural sources of gold anywhere in that country, but this fact did not prevent the Sumerian goldsmiths from developing great skill in working the metal they got in abundance from foreign lands—though, strictly speaking, *abundance* is not the word that leaps to mind in connection with the land of Ur, today's Iraq. It was not and is not a smiling, fertile country. Though the name Mesopotamia means "land between rivers," those rivers, the Tigris and Euphrates, did not, like the Nile, bring much benefit to the land they drained.

In early days, three thousand years before Abraham lived at Ur (his dates are c. 1800 B.C. to 1757 B.C.), the early settlers of Mesopotamia were wiped out, with their flocks and crops, by Noah's great flood. Later more immigrants appeared, people who, unlike their pastoral predecessors, understood the working of metal and other arts of civilization. A rich and luxurious people, they buried their kings in the Mesopotamian Valley in elaborate tombs with, to quote the *Encyclopedia Britannica,* "almost incredible treasures in gold, silver, bronze, and semi-precious stones," as well as princely retinues of officials, servants, and women, who evidently all sacrificed themselves willingly to join their monarchs underground. The survivors made literate records of religious rites and metallurgical expertise on clay tablets and buried them with musical instruments, weapons of gold, engraved shell plaques, mosaic pictures, statuary, and carved cylinder seals: A whole civilization was hidden beneath the desert surface until modern archaeologists disinterred it. In a suburb of Ur the diggers found more treasure, with proof that the legendary Sargon of Akkade did indeed rule over this land in the 24th century B.C., when Ur commanded the seaport of Dalmen, now Bahrain. Here the sea-kings of Ur, says the *Encyclopedia,* "carried goods for export . . . and there [at Bahrain] picked up the gold and hardwood, the ivory, and the silver that came from the Far East." In other words, from India.

The gold that arrived through this gateway was handled by goldsmiths who were astonishingly expert in their craft. The metal was purified by methods such as cupellation, still in use today. (Cupellation is the refinement of gold in a porous cup, or cupel.) The famous "lost-wax" process, modeling an object in wax, casting it, and melting out the model, was employed by these artisans, who were also conversant with annealing, the setting of precious stones, and gilding. There is evidence that gilding in particular played a large part in the glories of Babylonian building.

It was in the remains of the third dynasty of Babylonia, from the twenty-first to the twentieth centuries B.C., that archaeologists found the famous ziggurat of Ur. A ziggurat is a distinctive kind of temple tower of stepped-back stories, a pyramid of receding block forms usually made of the glazed brick characteristic of Mesopotamian architecture. The Tower of Babel, or Babylon, was such an edifice. Something similar can be seen today in certain buildings in Moscow, and perhaps in Mexican pyramids, but nowhere else that I know of, and in Moscow, at least, they are obviously merely an architectural conceit, certainly not built for purposes of worship. Gold in abundance was used in the decoration of the Babylonian ziggurats.

In time these buildings became the shapeless lumps on the empty Iraqi landscape that faced the archaeological team brought by C. Leonard Woolley to investigate Ur. Every last vestige of gilding had of course disappeared. It must have been hard for the team to believe that Ur was ever a thriving community housed in comfortable, well-constructed, two-story buildings almost exactly like the better-class Arab house of today. But the treasures produced by the excavations were dramatically convincing.

2

SCYTHIAN AND
OTHER GOLDSMITHS

Herodotus, the so-called Father of History, visited Babylon during one of his many journeys from his native Halicarnassus, probably going there by way of a boat down the Euphrates, some time
after 454 B.C. He is a charming commentator and a valuable
source of information about the world he knew. Scholars, as
scholars will, have long argued about him and his dependability.
Certainly some of what he said is open to question, but like Marco
Polo he has sometimes been unjustly accused of lying when what
he did was simply report the strange things he saw and heard.
For our purposes he is exceedingly useful, because he was fascinated by gold and wrote a good deal about it.

In Herodotus's day, Babylon, not far west of Ur, was the capital
city of Mesopotamia, the government having moved there from
Nineveh after that city fell to the Persian invader Cyrus in 538
B.C. Herodotus described it as a vast city in the form of a square
with sides nearly fourteen miles long and a circuit of some fifty-
six miles. It was surrounded by a broad, deep moat, within which
was a wall of baked brick stuck together with mortar. Along the
top of the wall was a row of one-story buildings and a road wide
enough for four-horse chariots. A hundred bronze gates were set
into the wall's circuit, and there was a second wall within. Babylon was divided into halves, each with its own fortress: One of
these was the royal palace and the other the famous temple of
Bel, "the Babylonian Zeus," as Herodotus explains. One reached
the topmost tower—there were eight of them piled up, one on

top of the other—by a spiral staircase. On the summit was a temple "with a fine large couch in it, richly covered, and a golden table beside it." There was no image here, but an Assyrian woman of the god Bel's choice (according to the Chaldean priests) lived in the room.

"The Chaldeans also say—though I do not believe them—that the god enters the temple in person and takes his rest upon the bed," wrote Herodotus. " . . . In the temple of Babylon there is a second shrine lower down, in which is a great sitting figure of Bel, all of gold on a golden throne, supported on a base of gold, with a golden table standing beside it. I was told by the Chaldeans that, to make all this, more than twenty-two tons of gold were used." (This quantity seems reasonable, considering that gold is so heavy that one cubic foot weighs about half a ton.)

Herodotus went on to describe a golden altar that stood outside for the sacrifices of such small animals as young lambs. He continued, "In the time of Cyrus there was also in this sacred building a solid gold statue of a man some fifteen feet high—I have this on the authority of the Chaldeans, though I never saw it myself." This statue was taken away by Cyrus's grandson Xerxes or Ahasuerus (519–465 B.C.), who killed a priest when the priest tried to prevent the sacrilege. All this, of course, is such a far cry from the ancients who founded the city that it seems practically modern, but even Babylon was not to endure beyond the age of Herodotus. When Alexander of Macedon (Alexander the Great) died, the city lost its position as Mesopotamia's capital. On the surface of the earth the temples moldered away, while beneath, in forgotten graves, its ancient treasure waited to be rediscovered centuries later.

But then, we can say the same of many other countries not all that far from Mesopotamia—Crete, for one; Egypt, of course; and Herodotus's own Greece. And there are many others. A few years ago, at New York's Metropolitan Museum of Art, there was an exhibition of golden artifacts, a glorious blaze of a display entitled "From the Lands of the Scythians," in which the public was given the chance to see treasures from museums of the USSR. They date from 1000 B.C. to 100 B.C., a long, long stretch of time.

Oh, this is it, I thought as I stood in the middle of one of the rooms. This is the color gold ought to be. Happily I regarded a kneeling golden stag, a large plaque like a cutout in bas-relief, about a foot long. Its antlers were conventionalized like a great curly mane lying along its spine from head to tail, feet together, head lifted. The catalog told me that this animal was found in a tomb between the Black and Caspian seas and dated from the late seventh or early sixth century B.C. When found it was lying on an iron shield that it must have originally decorated, "one of the few instances in which it is absolutely certain how the Scythians used such large, animal-shaped plaques."

Another animal in the collection, also represented in a plaque, in the same position and from the same century (or approximately the same century) is a golden panther, the tail and paws of which, when one looks at them closely, are perceived to be made up of many, many more little cat animals strung together in a cunning design. Obviously these patterns mean more than the simple outpouring of some artist's impulse, but what? Were they of religious significance? Very likely. Russian archaeologists who have studied them are not sure if the often-repeated motifs of stag and panther are supposed to represent dead or living animals. The facial expressions are alert as if alive, but the feet are always placed together, as they would be if the dead body were swung on a pole between carriers. But the large stag, especially, looks so alive it is hard to believe it was not meant to be.

Before going to the exhibition I had cheerfully assumed, as one does in such cases, that I knew who the Scythians were, but I soon found out that I didn't. The guidebook filled me in to some extent, saying that they were "an Iranian-speaking people, one of the many groups of nomads who dominated the Russian steppe during the first millennium B.C." These particular nomads occupied the territory north of the Black Sea and had very probably come there from Siberia, moving gradually west, in the late seventh century B.C., into the Pontic steppes. In the catalog were large, tantalizing excerpts from Herodotus, and after reading this text I went and got hold of his whole book. I soon realized that what we have in common is, first and foremost, an interest in gold. He liked it splashy and plentiful, as it was in Babylon. He admired Croesus, especially, because the Lydian king had so much of it. Croesus's wealth, like that of his father, Alyattes, probably came for the most part from the Ural and Altai mountains of Siberia, the miners simply washing the water that came down in streams from the highlands. One of Herodotus's translators said, in a footnote, "Altai is said to be derived from a Tatar word signifying gold." However Croesus got it—apart, of course, from inheriting it—gold enabled him to raise the standard of gifts made by his royal house to the temples of those gods credited with showering blessings on him and his family, usually in the form of victory in battle.

By custom these offerings were bestowed on the shrines involved through the medium of the priests or seeresses who tended them. Apollo's famous temple at Delphi was under the management of the Pythia, an oracle who was often called on to prophesy in reply to the anxious questions of important officials. According to an outmoded belief, when one of these individuals posed such a question the seeress would place her three-legged stool inside a little holy cell, chew some laurel leaves, and under their intoxication (presumably) would then make her oracular pronouncements. Another school held that she did not chew laurel but depended for inspiration on gases that emanated from a crack in the rocky ground over which she placed the stool. Neither of these tales is the truth. The Pythia did not operate alone but had her advisers, and, like members of the British House of Commons, the whole advisory body took notice of the public's questions some days ahead of time. Then, again like question time at the Commons, they replied with communications prepared in advance. The reply came via the voice of the Pythia, as it does through the voice of the appropriate Minister in London today, but there was a difference. The oracle's replies were oracular; that is, they were usually cryptic, couched in obscure imagery and riddles impossible for amateurs to understand. But seekers after wisdom had to be satisfied with what they got; if they weren't satisfied, they went to interpreters to help them out. Around these interpreters quite a flourishing secondary industry grew up. Whether or not the messages seemed to promise good things, the visitors were expected to pay Apollo handsomely by bestowing on the oracle or her representative sacrifices of animals and gifts of value.

Until one of Croesus's predecessors, King Gyges, set a grander style in such gifts, they had usually consisted of ordinary chalices and images. Gyges, however, showered the Delphic shrine with gold and silver objects, and King Midas (the real one, not the legendary figure), who came after him, presented the Pythia with his own splendid judgment seat, which was set up on display in the temple of Apollo. When it was Croesus's time he outdid all these benefactors. In his desire to please the Apollo of Delphi he arranged a magnificent sacrifice of 3,000 assorted beasts and also heaped up a quantity of rich objects—couches inlaid with gold, golden goblets, and splendid gold-embroidered clothes, all of which were set afire and burned to cinders, or perhaps slag and nuggets. Furthermore, having collected a lot of gold in taxes from the Lydians, he had it all melted down and cast in the form of 117 ingots, or bars, eighteen by nine by three inches in size. Four of these were of the best refined gold, weighing 142 pounds apiece. The rest, made of alloyed gold, were a little lighter—114 pounds.

Croesus's smiths also made a golden lion of refined metal that weighed 570 pounds. Later, when the Delphic temple was burned down, the lion toppled off its golden base and melted somewhat, losing 200 pounds' worth of gold, but it was still on view in the Corinthian treasury at Delphi when Herodotus paid the place a visit, and he saw it there. He also saw two huge mixing bowls Croesus had sent to Apollo's shrine, one of gold and the other of silver; the golden bowl weighed nearly 500 pounds. Croesus sent other precious things, but one of the chief wonders among his gifts was a golden statue four and a half feet high, said to be a portrait of the woman who baked the king's bread. As an afterthought Croesus included in his offerings his own wife's jewels.

Yet all this splendid treasure did not bring Croesus what he wanted: a good augury for his project of conquering his enemy, the Persian king Cyrus. The oracular pronouncement *might* have promised him success if one read it in a certain way, but in fact, as he realized too late, it carried a warning which Croesus did not recognize. That is the trouble with oracles: They can be interpreted in at least two ways, as anyone who has ever visited a fortune-teller will admit. What the prophecy actually said was that Croesus, if he went ahead with his plans, would destroy a great nation. Fine, he naturally thought; I'll destroy Cyrus's kingdom of Persia. So he went ahead and, sure enough, a great nation was destroyed, but it was his own nation that went under, and all the gold in the shrine of Apollo did not change the facts. Which hardly seems fair, especially as Croesus had also given similar presents to another shrine in Milesia and various splendid golden offerings to a number of different temples. At Ephesus, for example, the priests received from him golden heifers and golden pillars, and he sent a golden tripod to the Ismenian Apollo at Thebes. But in spite of all this, Cyrus defeated the Lydian troops and spared Croesus's life only because he admired his intelligence. Croesus became an adviser to his erstwhile enemy and accompanied him on all his later expeditions.

No doubt Herodotus heard about all these old, past campaigns from people whose fathers and grandfathers had taken part in the wars. We know that he lived for a while on the Black Sea, in a city called Olbia on the sea's north coast near what today we call the Sea of Azov, a district that was well acquainted with Scythian peoples and not far, it seems, from their fellow nomads, the Massagetae. Herodotus wrote at length about the Massagetae because he was telling his readers about Cyrus and the Persian conquests, and Cyrus, having conquered Assyria, turned his attention to them. He said they lived north of Babylonia and the Araxes (or Volga) River, in what we nowadays call Armenia, and could also be found to the east of the Caspian Sea, in the wide country to the north of the great stretch of land known as the Persian Empire. In the war that followed Cyrus's attack on these Massagetae, the Massagetae were victorious over the Persians, and Cyrus himself was killed.

But who were they, this savage people who vanquished such a powerful leader and his troops? Herodotus said they were a tribe who dressed and lived like the Scythians. They were completely at home on horseback but could also fight just as fiercely on foot. The only metals they used were gold and bronze—bronze for their spearheads, arrow points, and bills, or pikes; gold for headgear, belts, and girdles. For their horses they made bronze breastplates and used gold for the bridle, bit, and cheekpieces. Silver and iron were unknown to them. One of Herodotus's translators comments that this seems to be perfectly true: Golden utensils are frequently found in tumuli, or rock heaps, of the steppe regions along with brass weapons, but there is never anything made of iron.

However, it was the Scythians rather than their relatives the Massagetae who fascinated Herodotus, and there in Olbia, just next door, he heard a lot about them. Not so long before his arrival in the port city, a mere three decades or so, they had actually invaded the country of the Medes and defeated the Persians on their own ground. Returning home, they found themselves embarked on yet another struggle, because their women, tired of waiting for them, had married their household slaves. The slaves, unwilling to give up their new power, refused to abdicate, and a war was on. The Scyths had to fight their way back into their homes, but in the end they succeeded and were once more installed. Herodotus detailed customs of theirs that seemed strange to him. The Scyths, he said, lived on a concoction of mare's milk, which sounds something like yogurt. They believed their tribe to have been founded by a man named Targitaus, before whose advent their country had been uninhabited desert.

"I do not believe the story [of Targitaus's origins], but it is told nevertheless," said the historian cautiously. Targitaus, according to the tale, was the son of Zeus and a daughter of the Borysthenes. With this woman Targitaus begot three sons, Leipoxais, Arpoxais, and Coloxais, the youngest. One day there fell from the sky four golden implements: a plow, a yoke, a battle-ax, and a drinking cup. The eldest son, Leipoxais, was the first to see these wonderful things and went over to pick them up, but as he got close they blazed as if with fire and he recoiled. The second brother then tried to take hold of them, but he too was repulsed by the flames. However, when the youngest brother, Coloxais, made the attempt, the gold did not blaze and he was able to pick up all four objects and carry them home. His two brothers were so impressed that they declared the kingdom to be rightfully his. All three of them, however, were considered to be founders of the Scythian race.

The extent of their country was so great that Coloxais, who had three sons, was easily able to divide it into three kingdoms, in the largest of which he kept and guarded the divine gold. For a thousand years after Targitaus first settled Scythia the gold was never unguarded; it was still there, according to the Scyths who told Herodotus their story, and nobody could very well contradict them because the extreme north regions of Scythia defied exploration. Vision was always blurred, they told Herodotus, by falling feathers that filled the air, rendering a good view of the landscape impossible. But Herodotus was not fooled. The so-called feathers, he wrote, were really snow, and the Scythian version of their origins need not be taken too seriously; the Pontic Greeks Herodotus met in Olbia had quite a different story.

What they said was this: Heracles (or Hercules) had to visit the country of the Scyths when it was still a complete desert. He did so because he was working out one of the famous twelve labors set upon him, carrying off the cows of Geryon from beyond the Pillars of Hercules on the ocean, a place better known to us as Gibraltar. Geryon lived on the island Erythia on the other side of the Pillars, near Cades (Cadiz) on the coast of the ocean, which (said Herodotus) was believed to be a great river running all around the world, though as he commented, there was no proof of this.

In the country later known as Scythia, Hercules found it bitterly cold. He unharnessed the mares that drew his chariot, drew up his lion's skin, and fell asleep. When he woke up the mares had disappeared, which surprised him because they never strayed ordinarily. He went in search of them until he reached a grassy steppeland called the Woodland, north of the Crimea; there he encountered a strange creature, a woman from the buttocks up, a serpent from the buttocks down. Hercules asked her if she had seen his mares; she replied that she had them safe but would give them back only on condition that he go to bed with her. Hercules did so readily enough, but afterward she was reluctant to fulfill her part of the bargain. It was only after some time, when he insisted, that she gave in.

"Very well," she said, "but you must tell me what I am to do with the three sons I now have by you in my womb. When they have grown up shall I send them to you or keep them here in my country?"

Hercules handed her one of the two bows he always carried with him, and his girdle, which had a little gold cup attached to the buckle. He said, "Whichever of the boys can put on this girdle and bend this bow should be settled here with you, in your country. If any of them cannot bend the bow, send him away." Whereupon the snake-woman restored the mares to him, and Hercules departed on his errand.

In due course the boys were tested, and only one, named Scythes, was able to bend his father's bow and wear the girdle. The two others had to leave the Woodland, but Scythes remained as chief of the Scythians, and because of the golden goblet attached to his girdle's buckle, every Scyth warrior thereafter carried at his waist a golden cup.

For his part, Herodotus, who was always uneasy with such fables, said he didn't believe either of the stories. He preferred another version about the origin of the Scyths, according to which they had originally lived in Asia and had fought with, and been defeated by, the Massagetae, who drove them across the Volga into the Crimea. But where had they got all their gold? Some of the Olbians told him that a one-eyed tribe called the Arimaspians lived in the mysterious northern regions and guarded untold masses of the precious metal which they had stolen from the griffins, "but here too I am incredulous," said Herodotus, "and cannot persuade myself that there is a race of men born with one eye, who in all else resemble the rest of mankind." Still, he added, it does seem to be true that countries on the edge of the inhabited world produce the rarest and most beautiful things. He was probably thinking of the Scyths when he wrote this, the Scyths and their beautiful golden artifacts which were made—though he didn't know it—from the gold of Siberia and not that of the griffins. (Who, or what, were the griffins? Evidently they were a favorite motif of the Scyths, because they are represented in many of the tombs that have been excavated in comparatively recent times, long after Herodotus. They look more like winged, bird-headed lions than anything else and are possibly derived from Assyrian designs.)

Although Herodotus was incredulous when it came to believing in a race of one-eyed Arimaspians, his caution did not prevent him from swallowing a remarkable story about India. Perhaps, as has been suggested, he didn't get it right because his knowledge of foreign languages was often faulty. At any rate, when telling about the Persian king Darius, who succeeded Cambyses, who succeeded Cyrus, he reported the following very tall story:

Among Darius's vast revenues when he was at the height of his prosperity (his dominion, Herodotus reminds us, extended over the whole of Asia with the exception of Arabia) was the tribute paid by the Indians, 360 Babylonian talents of gold dust every year. Here it must be explained that people of that time used two units of weight; the Babylonian talent and the Euboean talent. A Euboean talent in Herodotus's time amounted to 6,000 drachmas. "A fine of 50 talents was a crippling burden on a large estate," wrote the editor of my edition of Herodotus, adding that one drachma per day was the average wage for a man on the crew of a trireme. Reduced to the Euboean scale, 360 talents of Babylonian gold would amount to 4,680 Euboean talents; thus the Indian tribute was a lot of gold. How, one might well ask, did they happen to have such a great amount of gold in India?

That country, Herodotus explained, was bordered on the east by a sandy desert. Among the many tribes of Indians was a particularly warlike group that lived very near the desert, in which was found a kind of ant of great size, bigger than a fox though not as big as a dog. Some specimens of these insects, he declared, had been caught and were kept in the Persian king's palace. Like other ants they dug holes to live in, throwing up sand in hills, but unlike the hills of lesser ants these were richly gold-bearing. In preparation for his collecting expeditions, each Indian harnessed three camels abreast, a female in the middle and a male on each side; the female camel must have given birth to an infant not too long beforehand. This was most important, as you will see.

Choosing their time with care, in the hottest part of the day, the gold miners rode their camels out to the anthills, where the ants were resting in the coolness underground. The Indians would leap off their saddles and start shoveling the auriferous sand into sacks they had brought with them as quickly as possible, for fear the ants, which could move very fast, would come after them. And so they did very soon, pouring furiously from their holes. Then the Indians slung their sacks of precious sand over their saddlebows, leaped on their steeds, and set out for home as fast as they could ride. By themselves male camels could not run speedily enough to outdistance the enraged insects, but the females, thinking of their young waiting for them at home, went

faster than fast, dragging their weaker partners with them. So the
Indian gold miners made good their escape, and the tribute for
Darius was safe for another year. At least, that is what Herodotus
believed.

3

AS IF IT HAD BEEN BRASS

I am looking back at late 1978. Christmas is on the way, and on a two-page spread in one of New York's luxury magazines is a selection of rich-looking articles headed PURE GOLD, a slight exaggeration since many of these artifacts are merely gold-trimmed, and not with pure gold, at that: They are fourteen- and eighteen-carat. One article is a lizard belt with golden buckle, loops, and tips; it costs about $3,200. (Do not forget that it's still 1978.) A gold cigarette case costs much the same, give or take $50. A gold lighter, eighteen-carat this time, is only $675, but a golden evening bag, caratage undivulged, is $37,000, which is pretty impressive. In 1978 you could have given your loved one a miniature golden license plate if you wanted to pay $300 for one of fourteen-carat gold. There was even a golden pocket calculator.

This is all far away and long ago now, but I remember distinctly that I was shocked, perhaps even horrified, by the prices. Thinking deep thoughts of conspicuous consumption I posed myself the question, Would the Thracians have approved? I mention them because their handiwork, being finer than that of the Scythians, is easy to distinguish.

Inevitably, Scythians and the neighboring Greeks, among whom Thracians are numbered, intermarried. At least one Scyth king took a Greek bride, and there must have been many Greek handmaidens in Scythian households, just as there were Scythian women acting as nurses among the Greeks. When people mingle thus, they exchange their particular arts and crafts; the Scythians, therefore, improved their knowledge of Greek goldsmithing.

During the last century B.C., when the Greeks still occupied
Olbia, their workmanship in gold was accepted as the ultimate
in artistic excellence, the best that could be found, and Scythians
as well as Persians set a high value on Greek slaves who knew the
secrets of the jeweler's studio. From these industrious workmen
came many of the treasures now housed in Russia's Hermitage
Museum, unless they have been borrowed for exhibition in other
national museums such as New York's Metropolitan.

Why Russia? How did the Russians manage to gather together
such a precious hoard? For one thing, they happen to live in the
right country for it: A lot of the crude metal is theirs to begin
with. Just how much gold is produced from the mines in the Altai
range is not known to the world outside, but the history of gold
mining in Russia goes back a long, long way, and like all stories
about buried treasure the tale of their worked gold is a romantic
one which I, for one, think rivals the account of the discovery of
Tutenkhamon's tomb. One of the best things about it is that there
is as yet no end in sight to the excavations. Consider what a wide
area is covered. Even Soviet Russia, vast as it is, doesn't contain
the entire tract of land that pays for investigation. Outside its
borders is Greece, where a significant cache has lately been
unearthed, but it is the history of Russian archaeology that I find
most fascinating. Dr. Boris Piotrovsky of the Hermitage has said
in his catalog for the "Lands of the Scythians" exposition that
"interest in the country's past had already begun in Russia as
early as the sixteenth century. Russian antiquities were being
gathered in the Kremlin's Armory Hall."

But the first real museum in Russia was founded in 1714 by that
inveterate collector Peter the Great. It was known as the Kunstkammer—the Private Museum, or Cabinet—and was stocked
with such natural wonders as mammoth bones and botanical
curiosities, anything a magpie kind of person like Peter might
pick up, as well as what were called antiquities. A year after the
Kunstkammer opened, a rich Russian, the owner of many gold
mines in Siberia, sent to his emperor, as a contribution to the
Cabinet, twenty "ancient gold objects" as they were described,
unearthed from kurgans, or ancient tombs, in that part of the
country. Then in 1716 the governor of Tobolsk sent fifty-six more
of these fascinating things from a similar source, and two years

later the government issued a decree commanding that a collection be made "from earth and water" of everything in Russia said to be unusual—inscriptions, weapons, dishes—in fact, antiquities in general. At the same time the official Academy of Sciences arranged and sent out expeditions to Siberia to do more excavating. Suddenly, after years of ignoring the kurgans, everyone was keen on examining them by shovel. Dr. Piotrovsky commented, "The director of the first expedition, D. Messerschmidt, mentioned in his diary for 1721 that digging up gold and silver from ancient graves had become a kind of trade in Siberia."

Soon the collection of gold objects became too big and important for a mere Kunstkammer to hang on to, and in 1723 the Academy of Sciences took it over. In 1859 it changed hands once more, being placed in the care of the Hermitage, which was then, as now, a museum, but at that time a museum in the private keeping of the Imperial Court. For a time after 1723 the flurry of excavation seems to have died down; furthermore, nobody ever bothered about other Russian kurgans that happened to lie outside of Siberia. However, they were too striking to ignore altogether, even though most of the natives of the districts involved (like those of our Midwest who live all their lives next door to Indian mounds but never investigate them) were not curious enough to see what lay inside the narrow shapes on which they plowed their fields or grazed their cattle. At last, in 1763, somebody dug up a kurgan in the Ukraine, and it turned out to be almost contemporaneous with Herodotus, of the late seventh or early sixth century B.C. It was a very rich find of gold and silver objects and included an iron sword in a scabbard on which were shown many golden animals as ornamentation. Nobody knew just where these things fitted in to the history of their civilization, however. "At that time the Scythian culture was unknown," Dr. Piotrovsky explained, "and the find was not fully appreciated."

In 1794 a Russian archaeologist discovered the ruins of an ancient city in the Ukraine, on the north coast of the Black Sea, and identified the place as Olbia, that settlement where Herodotus had lived and made notes on the Scyths. Olbia had been lost for centuries, but there it was, and more lore on the Scyths was forthcoming, though it was not brought out immediately. Thirty-six years later, in 1830, workers on a new construction project in that vicinity stumbled on a stone burial vault under a kurgan known as Kul Oba, also on the Black Sea and located on the straits that lead to the Sea of Azov. Official antiquarians were notified, and they hurried to the spot. When they saw what had been discovered, the new construction was forgotten. It was a splendid cache, attributed to the fourth century B.C., the burial of a Scythian chieftain with his wife and servant just as Herodotus had described such an interment. The chieftain wore a gold torque around his neck, and his wife was dressed in gold-ornamented clothes; arranged around the bones in the burial chamber were a number of other treasures. It was here that the diggers uncovered the great golden stag plaque, that same shield decoration that was a centerpiece of the exhibit at the New York Metropolitan Museum in 1975, and among the other things was an iron sword in a golden sheath. "If gold rust, what shall iron do?" Chaucer once asked, but this iron has held up pretty well.

In my edition of Herodotus a footnote described the contents of another kurgan excavated soon after this one: the skeletons of a man, a woman, and a horse, with weapons and rich ornaments in profusion. The human skeletons lay on sheets of pure gold and were covered with similar sheets, the entire weight of the four golden sheets being forty pounds. Golden utensils were found in another similar burial, among them a goblet weighing two and a quarter pounds.

Kurgans and the Black Sea were not the only sources of gold. Herodotus spoke of Carthage as another. The Carthaginians told him about a wonderful island called Cyrannis, near their coast, with a lake in the middle of it "from which the young maidens of the country drew up gold-dust, by dipping into the mud birds' feathers smeared with pitch. If this be true, I know not," he added with his customary caution, "but I write what is said."

The Carthaginians told him more on the same subject. They said there was a country in Libya, and a nation, beyond the Pillars of Hercules, which they often visited for purposes of trade, the Carthaginians being among the keenest traders of the ancient world. A certain routine had to be followed with these Libyan natives because they were so shy. The Carthaginians had to take the articles they wanted to sell and set them out on a beach, then go back to their ships and kindle fires so that the natives could see the smoke and understand what it meant. Then they would come down to the shore, look at the goods, put down whatever amount of gold they thought the things worth, and withdraw to a safe distance to wait. In their turn the Carthaginians came ashore again to check up. If they were satisfied with the gold payment they took it and went away; if not, they went aboard again and waited patiently for the customers to think things over and make another offer, until at last a bargain was struck—a very long-drawn-out haggle. The most remarkable thing about all this, remarked Herodotus, was that neither party ever cheated the other.

Another gold story told by the Father of History (or Father of Lies, as some have called him) is about an Athenian who rendered useful services to Croesus in a way that seems familiar to us. On the famous occasion when Croesus sent messengers to Delphi to consult Apollo's oracle, they were strangers to the place and naturally needed some friendly local person to help them out and advise them as to procedure. You and I would find it awkward if we went to, say, Washington, D.C., to interview a powerful official, especially in the tourist season, if we didn't have a friend or relative to show us the ropes. It was the same with the Lydian messengers, who would have been completely at sea if the friendly Athenian had not stepped in and aided them. He helped them to find lodgings in the crowded city and showed them the way to the shrine, which even today is a long way off from Athens. When they got home the messengers reported all this to Croesus, and the king appreciated the Athenian's helpfulness. Later, when the same Athenian came to Lydia and went to court, Croesus expressed his gratitude by telling his guest that he was to have the run of the famous royal treasure house, from which he could take away as much gold as he could carry.

Having made an appointment with the king's treasurer, the Athenian returned to his apartment and got ready. He put on a loose tunic that bagged at the waist and wore the biggest buskins he could find on his feet. In the treasure house he made his selection carefully. First he filled his buskins with gold dust, into which he painfully crammed his feet. Then he began filling the extra space in his baggy tunic with gold pieces, and when that held as much as he could cram into it he finished off by sprinkling gold dust in his hair and filling his mouth with gold. Emerging from the treasure house, he could scarcely waddle. Croesus, who was waiting outside, burst into laughter at the sight and awarded him with as much gold again as he had taken. The incident founded the fortunes of the Athenian's family, which in time became famous for its riches.

All this, of course, took place before the Persians attacked Greece and lost the war, forcing Xerxes to flee from the Greeks. Nearly all the other Persians, Herodotus proudly recorded, were slain on the battlefield. At the final rout a Persian general named Masistius was set upon by Athenian soldiers, who caught his horse on the field, knocked the rider to the ground, and tried to kill him. For a while they did not succeed and were mystified because their swords had no effect on his body. Masistius, in fact, was wearing a golden breastplate under his scarlet tunic, and it kept him safe until a soldier at last drove his weapon into the general's eye and so despatched him.

After the victory there was so much treasure involved that the Spartan general Pausanias had to adopt regulatory measures, announcing that to avert murderous quarrels there was to be no free-for-all for the booty, as there usually was during victory celebrations. The Greeks' helots, or slaves, were ordered to gather up all the gold and other treasures and bring them to an allotted place in the camp, there to be heaped up. The slaves accordingly went through the enemy tents looting whatever looked valuable, and of that there was plenty: "Many tents richly adorned with furniture of gold and silver," wrote Herodotus gloatingly; "many couches covered with plates of the same, and many golden bowls, goblets, and other drinking-vessels." They found bags of silver and golden kettles in the carriages and stripped the bodies of the dead of their bracelets, chains, and gold-trimmed scimitars. There was so much choice loot they didn't bother with such lesser valuables as the richly embroidered clothes of the corpses, but as they collected for the common herd they did not neglect their own interests, taking for themselves whatever valuables they could hide. Later they sold these things to the locals, who bought gold from the helots "as if it had been brass."

When at last the loot had all been heaped up, Pausanias took for himself a tenth of the gold and set it apart. Some later went into the making of a golden tripod destined for the temple at Delphi; some of it bought presents for the other gods of Olympus and the Isthmus. Pausanias also claimed and selected for himself ten women, ten horses, ten talents of money, ten camels, and so on. What remained was shared out among the soldiers—Persian concubines, gold, silver, beasts of burden, and other valuables—with due allowance made for those who had distinguished themselves by their valor. That was all, save for the belongings of Xerxes, which had been left untouched in a war tent that he had put in the care of his commanding general, Mardonius, when he himself ran away. Critically Pausanias inspected it in all its splendor; it was of course luxuriously furnished. Then the Spartan general called in the cooks and bakers who had customarily traveled with Xerxes and ordered them to serve up a typical banquet complete with "the couches of gold and silver daintily decked out with their rich couvertures," wrote Herodotus, "and the tables of gold and silver laid, and the feast itself prepared with all magnificence."

Pausanias also commanded his own retinue to prepare a Spartan supper to be served at the same time. When all was ready, he called in his officers and indicated to them the two meals, ready and waiting. "I sent for you, O Greeks, to show you the folly of this Median captain, who, when he enjoyed such fare as this, must needs come here to rob us of our penury."

Still, one must note that those penurious Greeks knew quite well what to do with gold when they got hold of it.

Today the journey to Delphi can be made by bus. A uniformed guide tells the party all about it, or a good deal at any rate, as the car full of tourists swoops around sharp curves and penetrates painlessly into the wooded mountains looking at the sea far away and below. At the site itself one walks wonderingly past ancient stones that dot the hillside. Some have obviously been worked, but with others one cannot be sure. Yes, here was a pathway and there the stadium, but of the cave that sheltered the Pythia and the gold offerings of kings there is no trace. Where, especially, is that inner chamber, the sacred spot where the oracle concealed herself with her advisers and composed teasing prophesies in reply to the people's eager questions? "Nobody knows exactly where she was," explains the guide. "There have been many earthquakes here since the ancient days. It is all different now. After all, it was a long time ago."

We stare in fascination at the rocky cliff where, at some unknown spot, the fate of powerful nations used to be decided. It was a long time ago indeed, though it rather surprised me to hear a Greek say so, but the fascination remains. Two news items in the London *Times*, published about a month apart and not much longer ago than yesterday, prove it. One, datelined from Athens on July 20, 1978, is headlined SIXTH CENTURY BC TREASURE ON DISPLAY IN DELPHI and continues:

A unique chryselephantine [i.e., combination ivory and gold] treasure from the sixth century BC, found by French archaeologists just before the outbreak of the Second World War, was put on display for the first time today in the museum of Delphi, near the spot where they were discovered some 40 years ago. The hoard includes two exceptionally beautiful heads of statues carved in ivory. They probably represent Apollo and Artemis. The god's curly hair is made of gold and he wears a headdress of long gold-leaf braids on either side. The goddess wears a gold diadem. Fragments include part of the goddess's right arm and hand which probably held a sceptre, her ivory feet and a profusion of gold ornaments and jewelry including headbands, bracelets, earrings and a necklace. There is also the left foot of Apollo and fragments of the other, a gold belt and, above all, the gold trappings of his robe finely embossed with animal figures. . . . Another outstanding discovery of the same hoard was a lifesize silver bull. It was made of hammered silver leaves that were nailed on a wooden frame that no longer exists. The animal's hooves, horns and genitals are gold plated. . . . The archaeologists found objects in ivory, gold, silver, bronze, and iron dumped together indiscriminately. They had clearly been damaged in a fire and probably discarded sometime in the fifth century BC. This dating tends to dismiss the theory that these valuable objects had been offered to Delphi by Croesus, the King of Lydia famous for his wealth. Since these objects had been buried in the fifth century BC, they could not have been among the treasures seen by Pausanias in Delphi in the second century AD, which he had attributed to the generosity of Croesus. The sculptures are probably the work of artists from Asia Minor in the archaic and early classical periods sent to Delphi as votive offerings by city-states in that region.

The other item, dated September 9, 1978, is signed by the *Times*'s archaeological correspondent and is headed VANI: INSPI-RATION FOR THE GOLDEN FLEECE? It begins:

The theory that Jason's land of the golden fleece, to which the Argonauts sailed perilously though successfully, lay at the eastern end of the Black Sea has received some support from recent discoveries in the Soviet Union. Excavations at the site of Vani, a fortified city in the hills of the Georgian SSR, which lay at the centre of the ancient kingdom of Colchis, have produced hundreds of pieces of elaborate gold work dating from the fifth century BC onwards. Most are jewelry.

This information was imparted to the International Congress of Classical Archaeology in London by a Russian archaeologist from the Institute of History at Tbilisi. The descriptions include those of a diadem with openwork front, necklaces adorned with animal effigies, and bracelets with animal-head terminals. Among the techniques employed were repoussé designs, filigree, and granulation. There were the familiar themes of warfare between animals—a lion attacking a bull, an ibex, or a wild boar; also, which is less common, a chariot with its driver and a necklace formed by a series of turtles. But I looked in vain for an explanation of what the golden fleece really was. No doubt the archaeological correspondent felt that it was too well known to merit repetition, but I don't think so. Therefore, here it is:

One of the oldest methods used in washing for gold, called *jigging* among miners for obvious reasons, is to run gold-dust-laden water down a gentle incline, joggling the incline as the water goes, to help the heavier metal settle on the bottom and encourage the water to move on. Gold miners of ancient days found that sheepskin was an excellent material with which to catch gold in this manner. (Today they use a similarly rough fabric if they can find it.) A fleece that was used in this manner for some time became heavy with the gold that stuck to it, and before it was dried and shaken out it must have sparkled in the most alluring—and precious—manner, a golden fleece well worth stealing.

4

THE COOL TOMBS

When Herodotus wrote about griffins (or gryphons) that guarded the gold treasure of the Altai, far beyond the other side of that land where snow fell like feathers, even he, with his enormous appetite for the marvelous, seemed a bit skeptical. But the men who actually lived in Siberia, where the Altai range separates their land from China, were very sure of what the monsters looked like, as we can be if we study the patterns and pictures brought from Siberia's frozen tombs. The tombs are a long way from being the kurgans left by the southern Scythians, but they are not dissimilar in many ways, except for the griffins, of which there are a lot about. After all, the people who constructed these tombs were nomads too, nomads of the steppes.

The frozen tombs have been preserved by the cold, thanks to which the belongings of the dead, even some made of perishable materials—wood, silk, and leather—have been kept in good condition amazingly long. There are among them artifacts that date back twenty-five hundred years.

"The finds from the Altai and from other areas of Siberia," wrote our old friend Boris Piotrovsky, snug, one hopes, in his office at the Hermitage, "show connections not only from the world of the Scythians but also with Persia and the Far East—connections which are illustrated in this exhibition by Achmaenemid textiles from Persia and silk fabric from China. The exhibition also contains fascinating objects of gold from the so-called 'Siberian Collection of Peter the Great,' excavated at the beginning of the eighteenth century."

I read this passage in the British Museum, where the exhibition was mounted for some months in 1979. Near the entrance of the rooms allotted to it stood a graphic representation of how the tombs came to be frozen and the powerful lords or chieftains preserved: not, one gathers, by deliberate human action but by climatic phenomena. After a tomb was constructed during early spring or autumn, the builders put a cairn, or heap of rocks, on top. A lens of permafrost promptly formed under the stones, as it always does at that season in that climate, and sealed the opening, because any warm air that remained in the tomb rose and deposited what moisture it held as soon as it reached the cairn.

"The cold air sinks," explained the description, "driving out the warm air and freezing everything." There all the tomb's contents remained, awaiting excavation centuries later. But at the time of burial, before any of this happened—the cairn and the freezing—there were ceremonies that involved marihuana parties:

The bodies were embalmed, the muscle tissues removed through incisions in the skin and the cavities left filled with grass before the incisions were sewn up with sinews. The skulls were trepanned to remove the brains. After the funeral there was a feast and a ritual cleansing by fumigation with the smoke of hemp seeds. Small tents were built of thin rods covered by a rug, and bronze censers filled with heated stones were placed inside. The mourners then clambered into the tent, threw hemp seeds onto the heated stones and inhaled the narcotic smoke.

Visiting the collections and reading these descriptions (not, I assure you, any breathing of hemp smoke) had an extraordinary effect on me. In the nights that followed I dreamed repeatedly of wandering through miles of cold gray halls, damp grainy walls facing me everywhere I looked. Everyone I encountered and talked with between these walls was dead, and I knew it, but the knowledge had no effect on our conversations. The prevailing mood of the party, however, was, to say the least, eerie. Whatever possible normality I was aware of in the dreams was held at bay by the griffins—griffins everywhere, holding up their heads haughtily. At best a griffin looks like a toucan in a bad temper, or an eagle with an abnormally large beak; at any rate it seems constantly rearing up in indignation. As I have said, a griffin does have an eagle's head as well as a lion's body; the dictionary is my authority. But the griffins of the Siberian frozen tombs cannot be quite orthodox in that respect: The bodies, whether those of lions or not, are not clearly defined. Besides, are there, or were there ever, lions in Siberia? I don't know, and I don't know, either, why I am spending so much time on this subject. Obviously it sticks in my mind; they were very vivid dreams.

Lions or no, there were certainly moose, or, as the English call them, elk. Like toucans, moose have very large noses, and the many moose among the Altai artifacts, in leather and wood, like the griffins, seem permanently affronted. Naturally what I noticed most of all, in my dreams and out of them, was the gold, that treasure which was guarded by griffins. There were beautiful golden articles from the frozen tombs, a bracelet of twelve coils for one—"representations in the round of a tiger attacking an elk," said the label, each animal stretched out in linear form; there were belt plaques, a belt slide, two golden buttons, and four gold strap ends. One of the plaques, modeled in gold and dated fifth to fourth century B.C., represents a restful scene done in openwork relief and is a little more than fifteen centimeters long. The catalog describes it in detail, justified if only because of the rare strangeness of the piece:

A man and a woman are seated under a tree, their legs folded under them in the "asiatic style." Another man is lying across their knees. The seated man holds the reins of two saddled and bridled war-horses. On the tree hangs a gorytus (a combined quiver and bow-case) with bow and arrows. The woman's head, seen in profile, is crowned by a high head-dress from which the two plaits of her hair rise up and are interlaced with the foliage of the tree. . . . The leaves on the tree, the human figures and the horses are portrayed in a state of peace and tranquillity. Possibly the subject is an illustration of a scene from an ancient epic, and may depict the resurrection of a dead warrior by his wife and his sworn battle comrade.

It was the final line of the description that I noticed particularly: "Instances of the resurrection of a dead warrior are known in ancient Turkish epics based on the traditions of earlier times." Noting that the piece dates from the fifth or fourth century B.C., I wondered how much earlier the times would have been. I knew that the Turks were in Asia a long, long time ago, so as soon as I had the chance I looked up the matter in the trusty *Encyclopedia Britannica,* where I read, "The earliest members of the present Turkey probably came from the Eurasian steppes of Central Asia." It figured. My golden earrings from Turkey look just a bit different from other earrings one sees—not quite like the gold pieces in the Frozen Tombs exhibit, of course, but to me at least they seemed special when I bought them, years ago, in Istanbul. However, they can hardly claim the originality shown by the goldsmiths of the Tombs. There, for one thing, they have a design described as a predatory animal attacking a snake in one of the golden belt plaques; the animal has a wolf's muzzle, clawed paws, and a very long tail. There is also a belt slide with the figure of a wolf crouched for a spring, which the catalog describes in detail:

The wolf's head, which has a long closed mouth, a turned-up nose, large protruding eyes framed by lids and brows in relief, and a well-modelled ear rests on its long-clawed fore-paws. A bird's head with a hooked beak decorates the end of the curved tail and other similar birds' heads are located on the animal's forehead and neck.

The wolf's face struck me as deliberately humorous, with a sly, sleepy, watchful expression caught by some artist exactly, all those hundreds of years ago, in gold. As for the ornamental birds' heads, they looked to me like griffins, but obviously I have griffins on the brain. Here and there were other, smaller bits of gold in the exhibit, even pinned or sewn to wooden and leather artifacts, like the so-called (by the Russian commentator) typical ancient Altai bridle made up of three straps: All the wooden adornments of the bridle were originally covered with gold leaf. I thought with sudden sympathy of the Scythian or Thracian goldsmiths, probably slaves, who hammered and hammered at their lumps of gold to stretch out the stuff until it was finer than this paper I'm writing on, until they had broad sheets of skin-thin, shimmering material. Not for them the heavy plates of Egyptian workmanship; this was on a higher plane of their art.

On the other hand, most of the elaborate gold pieces, such as the quiet tree with its seated figures and waiting horses, were cast. They show traces on their backs of woven patterns, ghosts of the material on which the gold was poured and then cooled.

One wonders, looking at these things, how the gold was collected that went into their making. We know very little about Siberian mines. A popular (and hopeful) theory is that there is still much gold in the Altai mountains; not long ago it was so plentiful (so the story goes) that it was enough for earlier prospectors simply to pan the mountain streams, collect alluvial gold, and sell it. Only lately, people say, have the Russian mine owners begun to dig beneath the surface of the earth and work the mother lodes, where abundant gold is found in veins that run through hard rock. But we don't really know. What we do know about gold generally we have learned in other places in the world, in Africa, India, California, South America, Spain, Alaska, Canada, Australia, Ireland. . . . It is a long list that includes both ancient and new gold, and rightly so, because in the end the age of the metal as we know it makes little or no difference. Any experienced smith can renew and remake it, change its color by combining it with other elements, and then, if he so wishes, purify it all over again. What he cannot do in paying amounts is to make gold from scratch. The time may come when he can, but so far nobody in real life can approach the feat of the dwarf Rumpelstiltskin, who easily transmuted straw into gold.

At this point we might think about diamonds and the long, weary time it took for men to learn how to reproduce the forces of nature and actually manufacture them. It was done at last, so that today so-called industrial diamonds can be made and sold, at a price. But even now it is cheaper in most cases to dig them up than to make them, and gem diamonds are even more costly and uncertain to manufacture. Those that have been made are too small to matter yet to the diamond trade. In any case it is hard to compare diamonds and gold, except that both substances are held precious by mankind. Gold is everywhere and diamonds are not. Gold can be extracted from many rocks—at a price. It is disseminated through seawater and can be concentrated from its colloidal form in the sea, but not in anything like paying amounts. The economics of gathering gold confront us almost everywhere we turn, with smooth, high, blank walls that cannot yet be surmounted; we must still depend on the ancient, toilful process of gold mining, or on the discovery of sunken galleons full of gold coins, or on more and yet more Siberian or Egyptian tombs, or —as our forebears could have told us in bitter detail—on alchemy.

The dream of the alchemist was to find the spell or method— or philosopher's stone, as it was often called—that would transmute baser substances into gold; for many years people, including the best minds in science—or what passed for science in ancient days—tried earnestly to do this. It is not hard to understand why, since so much depended and still depends on the possession of vast quantities of the mineral: success, authority, security, the happiness of nations, everything that has always been connected in our minds with wealth. It was not merely a question of keeping up with the man, or nation, next door. There is always another next door. The world's population grew, and the supply of gold did not keep up with that growth. That is why some very respectable and respected people were alchemists a long time before alchemy's child, chemistry, evolved from it and became the accepted branch of science that it is. Kings, savants, priests, even saints dabbled in alchemy, from motives not necessarily base. Admittedly, some of the alchemists were rascals, but many more were quite sincere, and from the studies they made of transmutation, even from their sometimes disastrous experiments, grew mineralogy, metallurgy, physics, and the related subjects that are now the main body of our scientific disciplines, including the great study of medicine. For a long time gold was believed to have important medical properties, and to some extent this is still true. Acupuncturists used golden needles; some still do. Certain physicians still advocate the use of colloidal gold in treating arthritis and heart trouble. Gold has its place in chemotherapy for the treatment of cancer, and it has been used, as its supporters point out, in space projects because of its peculiar reflecting qualities, which help to protect astronauts.

It is pleasant to remind ourselves that all the expenditure of thought, effort, and wealth, not to mention lives, has not been completely in vain. Today in the laboratory it is actually possible to "make" gold, though not exactly from scratch; at least it is possible to transmute something else into the noble metal. Indeed, there is more than one way to do this, but the simplest is probably as follows:

Take lead, which is near gold in the table of atomic weights, and bombard it with neutrons until it becomes a radioactive isotope of thallium, thallium being another element close to gold in the atomic table. You then bombard the thallium with more neutrons until it turns into its close relative mercury. Continue the process of bombardment until, in the third stage, you have gold. The drawback to this whole business is twofold. For one thing, gold got in this way is unstable, and in a short time will revert to one of its earlier forms. For another, the operations cost far more than the gold, even if it were stable, would be worth. Still, for what it is, there you have it, the answer to all the seeking of the alchemists: genuine, hundred-percent, lovely gold, fresh from the laboratory. And some day, when we know how to stabilize it and mass-produce it so it won't cost so much, who knows?

From Siberia in the days of the nomads down through the many ages of Greece and the conquests of Alexander of Macedon, gold rode high as a desirable object. When Rome supplanted Alexandria and the cities of Greece, gold was coveted more than ever; the conquerors learned to love it and collected it from any possible source. The capture of Spain, which had more gold mines than any of the other European countries, served for a long time to satisfy gold hunger, but the Romans never tired of going out to collect more. They found some in Gaul and more in the British Isles, where Irish gold was much prized, but the most valuable source was still Spain. There, the owners of the mines introduced hydraulic action and wreaked lasting havoc on the land: Wherever gold was scattered in friable rock and soil, they learned to collect it quickly by diverting streams and rivers onto the ground surface, pushing with such force that the earth was soon flushed away, well washed in the process, and picked clean of gold. In this fashion hills and mountains were washed into the sea; the topography of the Iberian peninsula was changed forever, of course at great cost to the people's agriculture. By this time, gold was being used extensively in coinage and travelled throughout the known world. It was now that the custom became widespread of "clipping," or taking tiny bites from the irregularly round coins, until the minters with their emperor employers invented the milled edge to prevent the practice. Of course counterfeiting, too, ran rampant, with gold leaf plastered on rounds of inferior metal. The chocolate coins covered with gold-colored paper now sold for children at Christmastime will give you the idea.

Much of the gold that came into the hands of the Romans passed out of their possession quickly because it was spent to purchase all the luxuries the known world could offer. Some of it went to China, which produced the silk they loved in Rome, but more traveled to India, where the appetite for gold has never been exceeded and never slaked. The emperors spent more and more, each trying to outdo his predecessors in extravagance. In the middle of the riotous spending, unnoticed save by a few religious Jews, Jesus Christ was born in the Near East, and lived and died scarcely noticed by the Romans, who killed him carelessly as one might a fly that was bothersome. A century after his birth, the Roman emperor Trajan tapped a new source of gold —for a while—when he conquered the country then called Dacia, now Romania and Transylvania, where there were gold mines. Some Transylvanian gold jewelry has been preserved. It is not unlike that of the Greco-Scythian style, but it is more sophisticated, as might be expected. Rome gobbled up that gold too. Taxes in the empire had to be paid in gold, but still there was not enough, never enough, in the imperial coffers.

The whirligig of time brings in his revenges. Another century and a half saw the Roman Empire much weakened by the savage attacks of barbarians from the north, and Roman gold trickled out in a steady stream to pay off the invaders, or to keep Roman generals happy in the provinces where they ruled like petty emperors. In the third century A.D. the emperor Diocletian gave up Rome altogether and moved his court to Asia Minor. Among other reforms, he regularized the empire's currency, which it badly needed. His successor, Constantine, who again moved the seat of government, this time as far as Stamboul (or Constantinople, as it was then called, after him) carried on the good work. Under him the accepted coin, known as the solidus, had to weigh a seventy-secondth of a pound, and this standard was so satisfactory that it held good for more than a thousand years.

By the time the empire of Rome and her successor in Constantinople gave up the ghost completely, in the fifth century A.D., the gold fever that had so long gripped her world was practically at an end. This does not mean that people no longer wanted it. They did, and gold never disappeared from the scene; for one thing, gold coins continued to be used as currency. But the long, fervid love affair was really over, and if it were not for gold's peculiar nature we might lament the centuries of waste that could be blamed on the Roman infatuation . . . though it was not exactly waste, was it? The gold was still there. It was somewhere, buried or otherwise concealed, disseminated, under new ownership, even lost, perhaps, at the bottom of the sea, forgotten here, unappreciated there—but the gold remained. Gold survives.

5

GOLD IN EUROPE

Gold survived, but the busy, greedy collecting of the metal that characterized the palmy days of Rome now faded into a general scattering of the wealth that already existed. For some years no new mines were discovered, and southern Europeans were left to hang on, if they could, to what they already had. The northern barbarians, in the meantime, were quick to imitate the Romans in the uses to which gold was put. They too coined golden money, passed it around as currency, and sought more of it. A logical development of ancient pagan offerings to the gods and goddesses of Egypt, Scythia, Greece, and Rome was that votive tributes were now to be found piled on the altars of the Christian God and his saints. Churches were enriched with gold; manuscripts were beautified with illuminated letters and pictures painted with gold leaf. Many a pious page gleamed with the precious metal and weighed heavy, as it was turned over to reveal still more gold. Vessels, crosses, and shields shone yellow in the light of church candles. Popes and cardinals wore gold-embroidered vestments and heavy jeweled golden rings, and secular princes were not slow to follow their example. To be sure, there was less showing off; the days of conspicuous consumption, at least outrageously conspicuous, were over, gone with dead Nero and the other emperors of Rome. But people still bought precious articles with gold coins and searched the mines of Spain for more of the metal.

We all have our favorites among the eras. Picking and choosing, as I have done for the past few years (there has been a great wealth of exhibitions of gold of one sort or another lately, and small wonder, considering what is happening in the world's gold market), I find that I tend to dwell most lovingly on the specimens recently revealed to us at the good old Metropolitan under the title "Treasures of Early Irish Art: 1500 B.C. to 1500 A.D." Some of these things are strange rather than beautiful, but all are fascinating; at any rate, beauty is a matter of fashion as well as taste. Unfortunately, a good deal of Irish gold design has been lost to us, because often when a cache of treasure was found in Ireland the finder would hurry to render it unrecognizable so that it could not be claimed. There is no telling how many lovely works of art were lost in the melting pot; gold has a comparatively low melting point, and it was all too easy to do. But some of it remains, and much of that was connected with the Church and so was protected.

Of course, long before the birth of Christianity there were gold mines in Ireland: G. Frank Mitchell, in the catalog of the "Treasures," declares that by 1200 B.C. Ireland, like central Europe, was part of the center of world metalworking. Irish smiths discovered how to make bronze by mixing tin that came from Cornwall with the copper in which their country abounded. Bronze was a far better metal for weapons than soft copper, and the Irish found they could exchange copper and gold objects for the tin they needed. For a while Ireland was prosperous: "Numerous caches of gold ornaments and bronze implements from this period show that there was a corresponding increase in wealth," wrote Mitchell.

But in time bronze was supplanted by iron as a material for weaponry, and by 600 B.C. the country's period of prosperity was over. Not until the invasion by the Romans in 55 B.C. was much more heard of the Irish. However, some of their gold ornaments remain, and even today they are found occasionally, heavy golden bracelets and the necklaces known as torcs. Look at this description of a torc (or torque) from the first century B.C., found in County Londonderry:

This splendid torc, of two conjoined half-hoops with a decorative fastener, is most elaborately made. The design, based on two interlocked sinuous curves, was worked by repoussé technique down the center of the two flat sheets of gold, leaving broad, plain margins. The design proper ends in a pair of balanced leaf motifs; the intervening curves form trumpets with lentoid mouths and foliage. In the spaces between the opposed curves are separately clipped-on bosses of relatively flat, well-defined spirals.

But it is no use going on without the illustration.

Christianity came to Ireland from Roman Britain, by way of missionaries, in the third century A.D.. In the fifth century the famous Saint Patrick arrived from England. Ireland's so-called Golden Age began three centuries later. In the catalog, Liam de Paor quotes an Irish storyteller's saga:

He saw a woman at the edge of a well, and she had a silver comb with gold ornaments. She was washing in a silver basin in which were four birds of gold, and bright little gems of purple carbuncle in the chasing of the basin. She wore a purple cloak of good fleece, held with silver brooches chased with gold, and a smock of green silk with gold embroidery. There were wonderful ornaments of animal design in gold and silver on her breast and shoulders. The sun shone upon her, so that men saw the gold gleaming in the sunshine against the green silk. There were two golden tresses on her head, plaited in four, with a ball at the end of every lock.

I should love to have seen her.

But it is in the Book of Kells, made in the middle of the eighth century, that gold really comes into its own. On these illuminated pages gold has been applied between, among, and around the strange figures that illustrate them. To manufacture the gold paint the artist mixed fine gold dust with white of egg and applied it to the vellum with exquisite care, using a brush of one hair.

Ireland was independent in her goldsmithing; the continent of Europe, farther south, was not. For centuries the southern Europeans worked along parallel lines. Italy's workmanship vied with that of France. Was Benvenuto Cellini, born in Florence in 1500, the greatest goldsmith of them all, as he firmly believed and wanted us to think? Perhaps not. Tastes and opinions change, as I have said, and this fact is pointed out by the translator in the foreword to Cellini's *Treatises on Goldsmithing and Sculpture,* C. R. Ashbee, who is severe in his judgments; he considers the

Neptune and Cybele of Cellini's famous saltcellar leaden and stiff. As a medalist, says Ashbee, Cellini lacked reserve and fine feeling, whereas "to estimate his position as a jeweller is all but impossible, as there is not one jewel remaining that can be authenticated as his." But here, relenting slightly, Mr. Ashbee admits that if we accept various pieces attributed to Cellini as genuine, he would be inclined to place him on an equal footing with any of the great masters of the early Renaissance or the Middle Ages in any country.

"Jewellery is, before all others, an art of limitations," he continues.

An artist cannot put less of himself into a gem than into a statue, he is necessarily more cabined. . . . I give therefore to Cellini as a jeweller an equal place with the artists of Greece and Japan, with those of Spain, England and Germany in the Middle Ages & the Renaissance . . . ; but as medalist, goldsmith and sculptor, I would place him on a much lower footing. My whole criticism might be summed up briefly thus: he was a very first-rate craftsman, but a very second-rate artist.

However this may be, it is thanks to Benvenuto Cellini that we know as much as we do about the glorious Florentine work of his time, whether it is his or some other artist's. His *Life,* one of the most enthralling autobiographies it is possible to find, takes in a good deal more than his various kinds of art—indeed, it is notorious for that breadth of subject—but anyone who cares about goldsmithing will find it worth reading if only for his comments on that subject, and naturally the *Treatises* concentrate on the technique of the studio and workshop. The book is still a valuable text for goldsmiths: Things do not change very much in that field. Benvenuto always wanted to be a goldsmith; it was an ambition he entertained from early youth, but he had to struggle for the right to do what he preferred. His father, like many other Florentines, was a man good with his hands; when he had to he too could turn out very creditable works of art in metal and wood, but he far preferred to make music, and he grudged his eldest son's spending time on anything but the flute. It was the fifteen-year-old Benvenuto, not his father, who found himself a place as apprentice with a goldsmith nicknamed Marcone; Benvenuto describes him as "a first-class craftsman and a very fine man."

The boy progressed well in spite of the fact that now and then he had to turn aside from his work to make music for his father, but this peaceful existence came to an end with the first of his many brawls. He had to leave Florence after this one, or at least it seemed tactful to do so. In Pisa he found another place with a goldsmith—and the pattern of his life was set. It was a very busy, noisy life, like others of the time, and should not concern us here except that he has been able to give us the best idea possible of what things were like for goldworkers in the sixteenth century. In the *Treatises* the directions are often reminiscent of certain cookbooks. Chapter 1, "On the Art of Niello," starts out, "Take an ounce of the finest silver, two ounces of copper well purified . . ." and so forth. (Niello, incidentally, is that kind of jewelry in which the object shows the gold or silver design against a black background.) In chapter 2, "On Filigree Work," the recipe is so exact that I, for one, feel that I could do it myself, though I certainly couldn't. For example, when Cellini is telling the reader how to place the wire into the desired shapes on the plate, he continues, "Now too much heat would move the wires you have woven out of place, so it is essential to take the greatest possible care—really it's quite impossible to tell it properly in writing: I could explain it all right enough by word of mouth, or better still show you how it's done,—still, come along—we'll try and go on as we started!" It is hard to believe that this voice rings out to us from the sixteenth century.

In 1541, in Paris where Cellini spent some years, he was shown a piece of work at court: King Francis I himself had sent for him in order to show him a number of pretty things, especially a drinking bowl of enamel and golden filigree so thin that the light shone through it. How, asked the king, could such a lovely thing be made? Cellini of course had the answer. First, he said, you make a bowl of thin sheet iron,

about the thickness of a knife back larger than the one you want ultimately to produce in filigree. Then, with a brush you paint it inside with a solution of fine clay, cloth shearings & Tripoli clay finely ground; then you take finely drawn gold wire of such a thickness as your wise-minded master may wish that of the bowl to be. This thread should be so thick that if you beat it out flat with a hammer on your clean little cup, it bends more readily in the width than otherwise, in such a way that it

may then be flattened out to a ribbon shape, two knife-blades broad, &
as thin as a sheet of paper.

He leads us in this manner through the whole process, soldering on the wire, painting the enamel, carefully firing the first
enamel coat, coating it again, firing it again, polishing it with
stones, then with finer stones, then with reed and clay, until, said
the king (as I just did), he really thought he could do it himself.
"And therewith he heaped great favours on me," ended Cellini
contentedly, "such as you can't possibly imagine."

Minuterie work, Cellini tells his readers in another chapter, is
all that class of work done with the punch—the work known as
repoussé, but cut down to a very delicate, small scale. "In my
time," he wrote, ". . . it was the custom, among other charming
things, to make little medals of gold which were worn in the hat
or the cap; and on these medals portraits were engraved in low
or half relief, and in the round, they looked just lovely." He
continued by saying that the greatest master of this art was a
smith known as Caradosso. He would make a little model of wax
in the form of the medal he wanted:

When he had carefully finished the modelling of this and filled in all
the undercutting, he made a cast of it in bronze of the proper thickness;
then he beat out a gold leaf rather thicker, if anything, in the middle,
and so as to admit of its being easily bent, and in surface two knife-backs
bigger than the surface of the model. This he proceeded to beat out into
a slightly curved form, and to soften with heat, and then laid on to the
bronze model, and with punches of the right sort,—wooden ones to
begin with of birch or dogwood, the latter by preference—he very, very
carefully followed the shape of his figure or whatever it was he was
working on. Ever so much care is necessary while doing this to prevent
the gold from splitting. And on you work, now with your wooden, now
with your steel punches, sometimes from the back, sometimes from the
front, ever most mindful to keep an equal thickness throughout, for if
it becomes thicker in one place than in another, the work would not
attain so fine a finish. It was just in this very getting of the gold so equal
all over that I never knew a man to beat Caradosso. Well, then, when
you've got your model worked up to the point of relief at which you
want to bring it, you begin with the greatest cunning to bring the gold
together over the legs and over the arms and round behind the heads
of the figures & the animals, then, if, when all has been well worked

together, there is still a little bit of gold loose at the edges, you carefully cut it off with a pair of scissors. And the little bits that stick out at the back of the legs and arms and heads, that is to say those in high relief, are likewise ever so carefully beaten down. By the way, I ought to have told you that your gold must be good, gold of at least twenty-two-and-a-half carats, but not quite twenty-three carat gold, for you'd find that a bit too soft to work in; and if it were less than twenty-two-and-a-half it would be too hard, and rather dangerous to solder.

With equally great detail and care he described how to make the solder: Take a little verdigris (copper acetate), absolutely fresh and as yet unused, salts of ammonia, and borax; pound these substances together and dissolve them in a glass of clear water. It turns into a substance like paint, says Cellini. This you spread with a soft wood shaving over all the joint lines of the work, pepper a little more well-pounded borax over the same places, light a fresh fire of partly consumed wood coal, and put your work on the fire. Be sure that your coals are set with their unconsumed sides away from the work as they are apt to smoke. Having put up a little grating of coal over the object, being careful that the charcoal does not touch it anywhere, wait until it begins to glow and grow red (or as he says, fire-colored), then blow wind over it with your bellows very gently and evenly, so that the flames play all round it alike. "If you blow too hard the fire will spring up and burst into flame, and you run the risk of melting and spoiling your work. When the outer skin of gold begins to glow and move, quickly sprinkle a little cold water over it with a brush. The soldering has been completed at this, the first firing."

There is of course a lot more to it than this, but it gives you the idea. Cellini would not have been Cellini if he hadn't been reminded, what with all this praise of Caradosso, of work he himself did in something of the same manner. A Florentine gentleman came to him with an order for a medal to give his lady-love. Expense was no object, he said. The subject was to be Atlas carrying the heavens on his back, but the actual design he left to Benvenuto.

"I set to work," wrote the goldsmith,

and made a little model with all the diligence I could, fashioning the Atlas in question out of white wax. Then . . . I determined to make a medal that should have a field of lapis lazuli, the heavens a ball of crystal, & engraven upon them the signs of the zodiac. So I made a plate of gold, and began, but by bit to work my figure up in relief with all the patience you can possibly imagine. I took a small rounded stake, and on this I wrought little by little, working up the gold from the ground with a small hammer, working right into arms and legs, & making all alike of equal thickness. In this manner, & with the greatest diligence and patience, I brought the work to completion. This we call "lavorare in tondo," working in the round; that is without putting the figure on pitch. . . . It wasn't till I'd worked it up to a certain point that I then took my punches and continued it on the stucco with very great finish. Then little by little did I raise the figure off its ground, which is a thing very difficult to explain how to do—still I'll tell you as best I can. Previously we saw how the arms & legs of the figure might be worked as one and part of the gold background, and thus make it possible for the background to be utilised as a fitting part of the design. Now, however, since the background is not needed as a part of the design, it may be used up; therefore with a small hammer on your little stake or anvil, & with the small end of the hammer you work gently on the gold, and with the action of the hand push the gold behind, using the punches as well, so that the figure comes up in high relief from the ground. . . . This is how I did the Atlas, & when I had finished him, I fixed him in those places where he was to touch the lapis lazuli background by means of fastening two little pins or stakes of gold, of sufficient strength, into holes made in the lapis, and so he was firmly set. Then I got a lovely crystal ball, of good proportion to my Atlas, engraved the zodiac thereon, and fixed it upon the nape of his neck, so that he held it high in his hands. To end all I made a most sumptuous frame adorned with gold, full of foliage, fruits, and other conceits, and set the whole of my work within it. Nor ought I to forget a very pretty sentiment that had to be added in the shape of a Latin motto.

In the course of time this medal fell into the hands of a connoisseur of such pretty things, who made a gift of it to the French king Francis I. The king was delighted with the medal and asked who had made it. Learning the name of Benvenuto Cellini, he decided that he wanted that master in his employ, and later, as we know from both the *Life* and the *Treatises,* Cellini did go to France to work for the king; he stayed there, working for his royal master, for four years. Before we discuss the most celebrated piece he ever made for the monarch—the saltcellar—it seems the time to describe one of the best known and ancient techniques in gold working, the lost-wax or *cire-perdue* method of casting. As far as can be ascertained, people all over the world, as long ago as the Scythians and even their predecessors in Siberia, knew how to cast gold in this way—except, perhaps, the Chinese; difficult as it is to believe, the people who invented printing blocks and gunpowder and paper and many other amenities did not work out the lost-wax process for themselves. It is only fair, however, to explain that they had another process for gold working that was just as good, perhaps better. To work their gold and cast it, the Chinese carved things—spheres, vases, anything solid—in rock, in half-forms, rather as if we should take orange peels and divide them into neat halves. They then carved the designs they wanted in obverse or intaglio inside these half-shells, bound the halves together with one end open, and through the opening poured their melted gold. When the gold had cooled and hardened, the rock shell enclosing it was chipped off. Making a golden cup was even simpler. A form of the wanted dimensions, made of rock, was sunk into a mass of melted gold. When it was removed along with the gold's container, or shell, the goldsmith had his cup—or vase, if that's what he intended to have. Of course a similar method could be used for plates.

The *cire-perdue* operation is different. The goldsmith makes a model in wax, which has been available ever since the first man robbed a beehive, and sticks into it at what seems the right position (or positions, if the article wanted is complicated), a funnel or funnels. Such a funnel is called a sprue and acts as a channel to carry off the wax when it is melted. There must be plenty of opportunity for the melting wax to escape; otherwise it will clog up and spoil the shape of the mold. In the simplest method, a shell of plaster or something similar is placed all the way around the model and the whole thing is then slowly baked. When the wax melts and runs out, what you have left is a hollow, shaped in the form you want to perpetuate in gold.

Next, the gold is melted. Pure gold, without alloy, melts at 1063° C., which is not very hot as minerals go. (It boils at nearly 3000° C.) This molten gold is poured into the shaped hollow and either cooled mechanically or left to cool naturally. When all is ready, the plaster coating can be chipped away and you are left with a golden replica of the original wax model. There are many refinements on this method and many variations on the underlying principle, but fundamentally it is always the same. Casting of this sort, as I said, was employed by a number of the ancients: the Thracians, the Irish, the Gauls, the Siberians, and any other people you might think of save for the Chinese and, oddly enough, the Peruvians, who used a method very like that of the Chinese. It must have been a case of parallel evolution.

6

GUATAVITA

There are many other ways to work gold, apart from casting. In Colombia the desired pattern is first portrayed in wood, which is then encrusted with gold. The gold object can be carefully removed and the same piece of carved wood used again and again. "They were into production in those days," said one of my informants, a modern goldsmith. "You could make pair after pair of the same earrings."

In those days! One of the most fascinating aspects of gold around the world is that the development of techniques, though they are sometimes strikingly similar when we compare them, is by no means simultaneous: There are considerable time lags. Take for instance the Columbian gold exhibition of November 1978, at the Royal Academy in London. As the invading Spaniards discovered in 1532, the Aztec goldsmiths were adept at alloying gold with copper—they called the resulting metal *tumbaga*—and were extremely skillful at casting. They made a sort of false filigree that was very hard to distinguish from the real thing made by European goldworkers. They made lost-wax figures and finished them off by hammering. With tumbaga figures, which might otherwise look dark, they learned how to bring out the color of the gold element in the mix by burnishing until it shone. They were expert at hammering and repoussé work. But look at the dates. Thousands of years are interposed between the gold work of the Siberian smiths represented in the frozen tombs and these Aztec specimens that were spared from rapacious Spanish destruction only four centuries ago. They were made, in all likelihood, about 1000 A.D. and saved (again like the Siberian artifacts) by burial.

The Royal Academy exhibition was built around one particular Colombian legend of El Dorado, which means the Golden or Gilded Man. Most of us know the story of the Spaniards who came to Peru in 1532 and could hardly believe their eyes when they found themselves surrounded by gold. Let David Attenborough describe it as he did in the Sunday *Times* Magazine of London, November 19, 1978:

In the capital city, Cuzco, the stone walls of the Temple of the Sun were plated with it. In the courtyards at festival time, the priests displayed life-sized models of llamas and men among trees filled with birds, all made from gold and set with emeralds and other precious stones. Even the pipes that circulated water through the palace were of gold.

Most of us, too, have heard the tragic story of Atahualpa, the Inca emperor who was incarcerated by the Spaniards. They said he must be ransomed with gold enough to fill his cell, a room twenty-two by seventeen feet and eight and a half feet high, and then, when the gold had been collected, they murdered him anyway. Having got as much gold as they could, the invaders broke up and destroyed most of the works of art so that they might the more easily send them back to Spain in the holds of their ships.

The Spanish colonists of the Caribbean heard about these riches and determined to find another source of South American gold, or at any rate another route to Peru. An official named Gonzalo Jimenez de Quesada, second in command to the governor of the island Santa Maria, thought it might be feasible to find the source of the Magdalena River, which he was sure was in Peru; the river would probably lead them, he argued, to the famous emerald mines in that country. He sent one party upriver by boat and took the main group, which included six hundred soldiers with eighty-five horses, a few priests, and some officials, overland to meet them at the river. Quesada discovered that they were not making their way through untouched forest; on the contrary, foreigners had been there before them. The party reached Muisca country, a tableland of Colombia where lived a tribe of very talented gold workers. There, sure enough, they came upon emerald mines and found the rich capital city of

Tunja, which, after their amiable Spanish custom, they sacked, taking as prize 150,000 pesos' worth of gold and 230 emeralds. There were other golden prizes, and tempting stories of a sacred circular lake known as Guatavita high in the mountains, which was rumored to hold an immense fortune in gold and precious stones. But before they could investigate further they heard worrying rumors that another party of Europeans, Germans this time, was also closing in on the treasure country, from another direction. Quesada's expedition took three years, 1536–39; the German explorer Nicholas Federmann was gone not quite so long, 1537–39. Between 1535 and 1538 another German explorer, Governor Georg Hohermuth, started from the Venezuelan plains to find the gold of Muisca. Sometimes it appeared that all Europe was hurrying to enter the act, but of these three, Quesada, after all, got there first. They decided not to fight but to combine and argue out their claims back in Europe when the time came.

All three expeditions had heard the same story about the Muisca and their gold. In actual fact there was no native Muiscan gold; the natives got all their precious metal from outside. It was what they did with it that was remarkable—that, and the fact that they treasured it as much as any Spaniard could. The expedition leaders also heard about El Dorado, whose coronation was inextricably tangled with the sacred lake Guatavita—had been, we should say, because by the time the conquerors arrived the custom had disappeared. Still, there were Muiscans who could remember the ceremonies; one in particular described them in convincing detail. When a new ruler was chosen, he said, the king-elect had to immure himself for several days alone in a cave, carefully refraining from salt, chili pepper, or any female company. When he came out, properly purified, his first task was to pay homage to the spirit of Lake Guatavita. On the lake's shore the people were busy preparing a festival and building a high, elaborate raft of rushes and trimming it with treasures. They loaded on it four braziers in which were burning a kind of incense, and the people who were highest in the land, dressed in their finest, embarked. In the middle of the raft were piled golden objects and heaps of jewels, especially emeralds.

In the meantime, the onlookers on the shore were busy lighting more incense and amassing piles of treasure, while over all were music and singing. Then the new king arrived, splendidly dressed, and the music swelled. He stood and permitted his attendants to remove his clothes until he was stark naked; then they rubbed him with resin until he was sticky all over and poured gold dust over him, rubbing it in so that it stuck to his body and gave him the appearance of a golden statue. He was ushered onto the raft, where he stood without moving as the boat was pushed to the middle of the round lake. There, to an even louder blare of trumpets, he began to throw his offerings into the lagoon, and all the people with him did likewise. The treasure splashed over the edge of the raft and sank beneath the water's surface: golden figures, coins, nuggets, emeralds and other jewels in their settings, gold plate, glittering adornment, bracelets, chains—everything one can imagine, sinking to the bottom of the lake. On shore, at the same time, the king's subjects were making their offerings—splash, splash, splash. At the end of the day, El Dorado returned to his palace.

That was the story the Spaniards and Germans were told, and they were avid to get to the lake and empty it, to get all the gold and jewels that, in their hopeful imagination, lay in the water. Somehow, though, it was not as easy as it sounded. For one thing, Guatavita (or Guatabita) was not easily accessible, and persuading the Indians to come along and work on draining the water was impossible. Quesada's lieutenant Lazaro Fonte tried, but ran out of money early in the game and had to give up. Then Quesada's brother, Hernan Perez de Quesada, tried, "in 1545 or thereabouts," according to the catalog. He had the good idea of waiting for the dry season, which lasted about three months, and he also managed to hire a number of laborers. They formed a chain gang and dipped the water out with jars made of gourds which were passed from hand to hand and emptied a good long distance away. In this fashion they managed to lower the lake's surface by about three meters, temporarily of course; the edges of the lake were uncovered and some gold was found: 3,000 to 4,000 pesos' worth. We are not told if this sum covered the expenses of the engineering, but the main idea, of draining the lake completely, fell through. There simply wasn't time to do it.

After that there were many attempts made by Spaniards, and

some of them, like Quesada, found some gold. But the true mother lode remained undiscovered, or at least covered, until the 1580s, when a rich merchant of Santa Fe de Bogotá, Antonio de Sepulveda, went at the problem scientifically. He built houses along the lake's edge, moved bodily to Guatavita, and went out repeatedly in a boat from which he took soundings. His idea was to drain the water by simply cutting through the rim of the bowl in which it lay. With eight thousand Indian laborers he actually got a trench cut through the rim, and the water started running out. The level was lowered by twenty meters, but then the trench fell in. Many Indians were killed and Sepulveda had to give up, but not before he collected from the uncovered lake margin more than 12,000 pesos of gold and at least one emerald of sixty grams in weight, which he sent to Philip II along with the king's share of the gold. Many of the gold pieces recovered were beautifully worked, though as we know the Spaniards did not consider workmanship as particularly valuable, being as they were preoccupied with pure weight. One historian records that Sepulveda found breastplates, or pectoral discs, serpents, eagles, and a staff covered with gold plaques and hung with little golden tubes. The merchant himself never made another attack on the drainage of Guatavita, though he often talked about it and was going to have another try when he died an old man and—as usually seems the case in these morality stories—poor. The cut he made in the lake's rim remained and can still be seen.

About forty years later, in 1625, a group of twelve men bitten by the gold bug petitioned the officials of Bogotá to let them try again to drain Guatavita. The officials agreed and drew up a contract by which the king was to get a quarter of the value of every thing found, "all the gold, silver, pearls, and other things of value," up to the worth of 50,000 pesos, after which His Majesty would be entitled to a half. Representatives of the crown were to oversee this division; the royal court had discovered through bitter experience that there had been a good deal of juggling done in earlier settlements of the sort. The consortium was allowed the use of Indian workmen, to be paid the same wages as soldiers, and had to promise to make good any damage done by the drainage to nearby properties. Perhaps the project was attempted, perhaps not; there is no record of it, at any rate.

Probably it never got off the ground. So there the lake remained, a romantic symbol, a source of dreams and nothing else, until in 1801 the explorer and naturalist Alexander von Humboldt visited Bogotá. Naturally he went and looked at Guatavita. He measured the slice taken out of the rim, took a good look at the surrounding mountains, and went home to Paris to do some calculations. Suppose, he wrote in 1807, a thousand pilgrims visited the lake every year. Suppose each pilgrim threw into the water five objects. How much would this treasure be worth by the time von Humboldt did his figuring? Let's see, he said to himself: That would make 500,000 offerings, which with a reasonable average worth came to $300 million in all. Calculating like this was a pleasant game and cost nothing. In a book published in 1825, a British naval officer, Captain Charles Stuart Cochrane, who had joined a company run by a rich man from Bogotá, Don "Pepe" (José Ignacio) Paris, did some deep thinking about the problem and raised the ante: "There ought to be gold and precious stones yet buried in it," he said of the lake, "to the amount of one billion one hundred and twenty millions sterling." Sterling! Of course, he and Don Pepe were especially interested in Lake Guatavita; they had designs on it.

At a party the captain gave a demonstration (this in 1823), before the vice-president of Colombia and other guests, of how the lake water could be siphoned off if all other methods proved useless. But it was half a joke to talk about siphoning, because he and his friend Paris thought the old-style method of cutting through the lake's rim was still the best way to go about their fortune hunting. The party and demonstration took place in September; on October 8, with the tunneling already in train, Captain Cochrane and Don Pepe went down to Guatavita to see how things were going. The answer was, not so well. The tunnel was within forty yards of the water, but it was in trouble: The sides kept slipping into the lake, leaving much work to be done again and again. The partners differed on their next methods of procedure, Cochrane arguing for shoring and planking, Paris against it because the process was running into too much money. Cochrane seems to have had his way, however. On October 16 he noted in his diary that things were going so slowly that he stepped in and took charge. On October 20 he wrote that he had made an arrangement with the government permitting him to dig in search of anthropological remains in the lake's vicinity, provided he gave the state 5 percent of the value of anything he might find. The results of these excavations were disappointing to the treasure seekers because, as he said, he found only pottery and bones. In fact, his efforts resulted in uncovering the first archaeological specimens of Colombia, something valued far higher nowadays than ordinary gold. Never mind; Cochrane soon turned back to his tunnel and reported on October 25 that it was finished. Now, he said, he decided to leave an opening so that the water might continue to run out all night. He figured that they could draw eight feet of water out of the lake in two or three days.

On the next morning the workers were gratified to discover that the lake level had indeed dropped six inches overnight, but the tunnel was again giving trouble, threatening to fill itself up with sliding soil. Cochrane gave orders to shore it up with more planking.

By November 12 the new planking was in place and water was running out in a satisfactory manner. The lake was now down ten feet and the tunnel had to be deepened so that draining could continue. Whether or not Cochrane was bored we do not know; perhaps he was over-confident. At any rate at this point he handed the job over to another man and went back to Bogotá. He died in 1824. In 1827 another British traveler summed up the story, which was not one of success. Paris and his company had tried for three years, he said, to build a tunnel that would do the job, but it was badly designed, being too steep in the walls; rocks and earth fell into it seven times. Losing heart at last, Paris accepted the suggestion of a friend that he should attack the lake from a point thirty feet lower than the lake bed and dig his tunnel underground. This effort very nearly succeeded, but some mishap (said the traveler) intervened at the last moment. The project was abandoned, and the company's shares dwindled to almost nothing.

But gold is gold, and there were some financiers who kept Guatavita in mind, until in 1898 a new company was formed with the old object of draining the lake. The moving spirit of this one was British: a resident of Colombia by the name of Hartley

Knowles, who bought the drainage rights of the company, promising to pay the former directors 41 percent of any treasure found. The story now becomes somewhat complicated, because Knowles quickly sold his rights to a British company, Contractors Ltd., who appointed him managing director at a salary (which doesn't sound very large—£25 a month) and a share in the profits. Contractors Ltd. was a joint stock company, and it sold shares at temptingly low prices so that poor people could help in the investments. A fish salesman in London, for instance, bought two five-shilling shares. The plan was to drive a tunnel up through the earth to the middle of the lake bottom, regulating the flow with sluices and catching whatever came out with the water on screens. It worked. That is, the water ran out and the lake bottom, for the first time in uncounted centuries—though lakes are comparatively short-lived—was exposed. Unfortunately for the exulting engineers, it was also very mucky, soft and slimy. Nobody could walk on it in safety, so the workers agreed to let it set for a while. By the next day the bright, harsh sun had baked it so hard that there was no question of digging into it with shovels. The company would have to drill, but it had no proper drilling equipment; it took time to obtain it, and when the equipment finally arrived, lake mud blocked the sluices and the tunnel, and Guatavita had filled up again to its original level.

To be sure, a certain amount of treasure had been recovered before disaster overtook the project: gold ornaments, emeralds, beads, and pottery. In 1910 some of these prizes, valued at £500, were sent to London to help raise more money for the company, which was running out of financing. So it went, with ups and downs, but more downs than ups, until the company gave up finally in 1929. There were other companies, other schemes, and other attempts, and more gold objects were found now and then, but in 1965 the Colombian government took over Guatavita at last and declared it part of the national cultural heritage.

The legend of El Dorado did not stop short with Lake Guatavita or, indeed, with Colombia itself. South American history is full of records of other explorers, beginning, as it is unnecessary to say, with Christopher Columbus, who did not visit what the catalog refers to as Caribbean Columbia until 1501–2, nine years after his first arrival in North America. The Spaniards

quickly found the gold they had always supposed to be somewhere in the Western hemisphere and busily settled along the
coast.

In 1512 Balboa had mouth-watering stories to repeat about a
cacique, or chieftain, named Dabeida, who was believed (by Balboa, at least) to control all the gold that came to the Gulf of
Uruba. Many Indians had told him, he said, that Dabeida pos-
sessed baskets of gold so heavy that a man could scarcely lift them
singly to his shoulders. He got the gold in the mountains two days'
journey away, where the people were "very Carib (i.e., savage)
and very bad." They ate human flesh. They also owned all the
gold, said Balboa, and they had two methods of getting it out:
Either they waited for seasonal flooding and then searched the
streambeds after the water had passed, picking up alluvial con-
centrations, or they burned over auriferous grounds and later
sauntered out to collect gold nuggets where they gleamed amid
the stubble. When they had the gold the Indians always brought
it to Dabeida, who paid for it with children (to eat) and women
for wives, and peccaries, fish, salt, and cloth made of cotton, not
to mention golden objects that they were not able to make for
themselves.

"This cacique Dabeida has a great place for melting gold in his
house, and he has a hundred men continuously working gold,"
wrote Balboa.

Fantastic as the account may seem, it happened to be largely
truthful, as later travelers were able to attest. Ferdinand II got
the reports in 1513–14 and decided to rename the area. Until
then the Spaniards had called it the Mainland, but now it was
changed to Golden Castille and appears under that name in a
1529 world map.

Balboa had started his journey from Darien, but the first genuine gold rush in Colombia originated in the province of Car-
tagena in 1534, under the provincial governor Pedro de Heredia.
The Spaniards there had concentrated on the lakes and savannas
of the Sinu; they did not even try to find original sources of gold
but simply dug up burial mounds. The more they dug up, the
more amazed and delighted they were with the rich booty thus
obtained. In two years, 1533 and 1534, they found 110 pounds
of fine gold and 53 pounds of "base" gold—probably alloyed with

copper. During the next three and a half years, under Heredia, the graves yielded 545 pounds of pure gold and more than 176 pounds of the lower-grade metal, and it should not be forgotten that this was the king's official report; no doubt the explorers found and smuggled more than that. In fact, by 1536 it was deemed necessary at the Spanish court to emphasize that the king, then Charles V, had a right to a fifth of whatever treasure was found, "metals, pearls, or stones, smelted or worked. . . . And of the remainder, the half of everything will be turned over to our Royal Treasury without any discount of anything, leaving the other half for the person who has found and discovered it."

These are clear directions, but it is not surprising that conditions deteriorated in spite of them. In 1537 the king found it necessary to send special instructions that "you shall not take gold from the sepulchres except in the presence of the Overseer, officials of His Majesty, or their Lieutenants." It was too late; almost all the tombs in Sinu had already been robbed.

One of the most striking items of the El Dorado exhibition was a Muisca figure of gold depicting the ceremony of the king who gave it its name. In this, a raft is made of golden wire or narrow bars, twisted around and around in an oval so that it has depth. The floor of the raft is made of woven patterns. The king, El Dorado himself, stands near the prow, his head decorated elaborately with a high headdress. Other smaller golden figures stand about, and there are bushes, or wheat shocks, of golden wire. I was staring at the pretty thing, which in all is not ten inches long, when I heard a child's voice behind me:

"But what is it, Daddy?"

"That's a king," said Daddy. "He's all covered with gold dust, and he goes out with his courtiers to the middle of the lake to throw treasure overboard."

"But why, Daddy?"

"Well," said Daddy, hesitating a little. "Well, so everybody who sees it will think, 'What a very splendid fellow!' "

"Oh," said the child. They moved away.

7

BRAZIL'S GOLD RUSH

To be quite frank, the exhibition of Peruvian gold at the Museum of Natural History in New York City in 1978 rather disappointed me. I admit freely that it was my own fault. As I have said more than once, I have preconceived ideas of gold and what it ought to look like: that particular color I have seen at times in sunsets, a light-diffused tint that is neither too dark nor too light for my ideal. The trouble, in my mind, with "Peru's Golden Treasures," as the exhibition was named, was that quite often they weren't golden at all. It seems that the Peruvians used alloys heavily and didn't mind if the wrong color came to the top; simply knowing that gold was there, evidently, was enough. Not that this was true of all the specimens. A mask, a pair of ceremonial arms and hands like golden elbow-length ball-gloves, a lizard in cast gold with round spangles for feet—these were very satisfying, but what was one to say of the mask with turquoise eyes and traces of red paint showing that the fundamental metal had been hidden even at the time it was made?

Many of the artifacts in the collection are fugitives from the Spanish soldier looters, criminal types who, led by Pizarro, kidnapped Atahualpa and cheated the Incas out of his ransom by keeping the gold and silver and then executing him anyway. Those treasures were ruthlessly melted down—it is a moot point which was the greater crime, treachery or vandalism—and sent as ingots to Spain, but before this calamity there was much golden beauty in the Inca civilization. In 1553 the Spanish soldiers saw the Inca temple to the sun in Cuzco—Coricancha, the golden enclosure. One of them described it, and is quoted in the museum's catalog:

It had many gates, and the gateways finely carved; halfway up the wall ran a stripe of gold two handspans wide and four fingers thick. The gateway and doors were covered with sheets of this metal. Inside there were four buildings, not very large, fashioned in the same way, and the walls inside and out were covered with gold, and the beams too. . . . In one of these houses, which was the richest, there was an image of the sun, of great size, made of gold, beautifully wrought and set with many precious stones. . . . There was a garden in which the earth was lumps of fine gold, and it was cunningly planted with stalks of corn that were of gold—stalks, leaves and ears. . . . Aside from this, there were more than 20 llamas of gold with their young, and the shepherds who guarded them, with their slings and staffs, all made of this metal. . . . In a word, it was one of the richest temples in the whole world.

And all this went under the hammer to be shipped back to Spain in misshapen lumps.

The Incas ruled for not much more than a century, 1450–1532; none of the gold work from South America has the antiquity of European and Asian metal. It was from the Chimu (1200–1470) that a lot of preserved artifacts have come, saved from the voracious Spanish because they were buried and hidden in tombs, from where, for instance, came the golden gloves and the funerary masks, which were tied to mummies. A passage from the catalog explains why I was disappointed in some of these things:

Detailed studies made at the Massachusetts Institute of Technology of masks similar to these show that they are not of pure gold but merely have a gilt surface. Far from reducing the value and interest of the masks, such studies underline the complex technology of ancient Andean metallurgy. Basically, Andean gilding worked by chemically removing the other metals (usually silver and copper) from the surface of a gold alloy, leaving an exterior layer of almost pure gold.

Gilding, of course, achieves a glittering golden expanse with a minimum of the precious metal. Economical use of gold no doubt played a role in the choice of gilding to make mummy masks and other large golden pieces. But still greater economies could have resulted from affixing gold foil to the surface of more common metal instead of beginning with, or in some cases producing, a gold alloy and enriching its surface by chemical means. On rare occasions that was actually done. One authority has suggested that ancient Peruvians may have felt the need for gold objects to contain some gold throughout. Their total "essence" had to be golden even if they consisted mostly of other

metals. And despite all the effort expended to achieve the golden surface of a mask, that surface was almost entirely covered with other
materials. Inlays of silver and other metals covered the flanges which
formed the ears; the eyes had insets of turquoise and other stones;
feathers adorned parts of the mask, and virtually the entire face was
often painted with materials such as cinnabar.

Why, the writer asked rhetorically, did they hide the gold? I
echoed the question fervently, and read on. "We come once
again to the important presence of gold throughout the object;
once the gold surface had been established, the fact that it could
not be seen appeared not to matter."

Except to me.

In fairness it should be remembered that the Peruvians and
other South Americans did not think of gold in quite the same
way as did the Europeans. They didn't think of making coins of
it, or even—with the exception of ransoming Atahualpa, and this
was taught to them by the Spaniards—of using it for barter. They
made ceremonial objects, sculptures, and, as we have seen,
golden gardens with golden cornstalks, livestock, and human
beings, but not coinage. The Spaniards brought the idea of coin-
ing money to America and promptly acted on it.

Much of the eastern half of the continent, of course, was not
Spanish at all, but Portuguese. The vast lands that had fallen to
these people through the decision of the Pope to divide up the
New World were not at first penetrated very far, Portuguese
immigrants being content to carve out estates for themselves
from coastal territory or to make their money through the sale
of slaves from Africa—"black gold," as they were called. Some
lorded it over plantations, on which they did very little manual
labor themselves. Only one group went inland, and it was these
men, the Paulistas as they were called (from the region of São
Paulo de Piratininga) who started the Brazilian gold rush.

"On the plateau of Piratininga, the colonists mated with Amerindian women to a greater extent than elsewhere," wrote C. R.
Boxer in *The Golden Age of Brazil, 1695–1750,* "and they

adopted much of the savages' jungle craft and forest lore. The Paulista
. . . was the South American equivalent of the French Canadian *métis*
or *coureur-des-bois.* More at home in the forest paths and bush trails of

the remote backlands than in their own houses, the Paulistas penetrated hundreds of miles inland in the course of their frequent expeditions in search of slaves, precious metals, and emeralds.

Late in the seventeenth century there was a financial crisis in Portugal and her American colony, Brazil. The home government, Brazilian planters complained, levied crippling duties on the goods they bought and sold in Portugal and Angola; as a result, smuggling was rampant. Portugal had been accustomed to buying silver bullion from Spain, which got it from the mines of Potosí in Bolivia, but the supply of this metal was falling off. Brazil's most important export crops, sugar and tobacco, were now less profitable than they had been. Everyone in the three-cornered trade between Portugal, Angola, and Brazil was short of actual cash, or coins. The governor-general of Brazil noted that in 1690 the colony had exported to Lisbon more than 80,000 cruzados. This state of affairs could not continue, he declared, without a crash, and in spite of all the home government could do, that crash seemed imminent unless some Brazilian stumbled on a mineral treasure equal to the Spaniards' silver mines. Accordingly, Brazil's adventurers made of themselves prospectors and set out to explore the hitherto unknown forest country that lay beyond the settled coastal strip bordering the southern Atlantic, what might be called the first true gold rush of the Americas.

There had been earlier attempts, of course, to match Spain's record. Brazilians, like Spanish settlers, had listened eagerly to tales of treasure like that of Guatavita and its El Dorado, and of all these the toughest, hardiest, and most determined were the Paulistas, offspring of colonists and Indian women. The Paulistas were admirably suited for prospecting. As sons of Amerindian women they spoke Tupí-Guaraní, the vernacular of the interior. Unlike the whites they were always on the move, and the interior held no terrors for them; "by 1651," wrote Boxer, "they had blazed trails to High Peru and through the dense forests of central Brazil to the Amazon delta." Their purpose in these treks through the highland region was the capture and enslavement of Indians to till their fields, but in the search they also kept an eye out for gold, silver, and emeralds, for some of them had already found some gold-bearing streams in Paranaguá.

Paulistas were also known as *bandeirantes*, owing to their custom of forming para-military groups like the Portuguese *bandeiras*, or militia. From their Amerindian attachés they learned so well how to cope in the bush that they became as good at it as the Indians who taught them. Some of them roamed the forest indefinitely, pausing when it suited them to grow crops of manioc, which they augmented as a diet with animals and birds (like as not killed with bow and arrow) as well as fish, berries, roots, honey, and other edible wild things. Says Boxer:

> Most modern representations of seventeenth-century Paulistas . . . depict them in a sort of "Pilgrim Father" attire with high jack boots; but in point of fact they seem to have worn little else but a broad-brimmed hat, beard, shirt, and drawers. They generally marched barefooted and in single file along jungle trails and bush paths, though they often carried a variety of weapons.

They also sometimes wore wadded cotton jerkins, very useful against Indian arrows. The central city of these hard-bitten men was São Paulo, which was isolated from the rest of Brazil by a mountain range, Serra do Mar; being hard to reach, it was a haven for deserters and criminals of all sorts who wanted to get out of the other settled regions. And it was the Paulistas who set seriously to work to find silver and emeralds in the interior in the 1680s and 1690s. Nobody else was tough enough.

Save for the alluvial gold deposits already mentioned, they had no luck at first, in spite of the fact that some of their bands moved over a lot of territory and searched it, they thought, thoroughly. But eventually they did make their strikes; not merely one, but more or less all at once in several localities, in the region now known as Minas Gerais, or General Mines. The first strike was made in 1682 by a Paulista named Manuel de Borba Gato. He was running away from the law, having been involved in an assassination, and in his flight he led his band to a hideout in the region of Rio das Velhas. It was a lucky choice, because the Paulistas found a profitable source in the river of alluvial gold. They tried to keep its whereabouts a secret, but the news leaked out to Rio de Janeiro and encouraged other prospectors. Other discoveries of alluvial gold soon followed. Not only the valley of the Rio das Velhas but also that of the Rio das Mortes and the Rio Doce all proved to be auriferous. Soon the rivers and the land between them were swarming with miners, who not only panned for gold in the water but stripped the land in their eager search.

The methods for mining placer gold are well known and much the same in any part of the world. The treasure seekers of Brazil used a slightly different sort of receptacle than the pan with which we are familiar in the western United States, but the principle was the same—separation by gravity. They would put their earth into a cone-shaped holder, in water, and swirl it around so that the gold nuggets and dust could settle to the bottom, leaving the lighter silt in suspension to be poured off. When a man was convinced that his particular portion of the stream had been worked until it was barren, he turned his attention to the banks of earth on either side, digging and washing it in the same way as long as he could hope for a profitable result. Only when the surface of the earth had been thoroughly sifted (and, incidentally, rendered bare of vegetation) did he move on. But some of the men, more intelligent than the others, reasoned that the alluvial gold must have come from somewhere higher up and not far off. It seemed wise to dig deeper until a man might chance to hit on the mother rock with—he hoped—veins of pure gold running through it. Sometimes he was right and found gold veins. The extraction of the metal in this case called for genuine mining, involving more sophisticated tools and greater investment. It is a classic procedure followed by the Brazilians' predecessors all over the world—in Spain, Egypt, Siberia—everywhere that gold has ever been found. The gold is usually contained in quartz, which in its turn makes up part of the native rock (igneous or metamorphosed) and must be pursued underground as deep as a miner's equipment makes possible. When at last the golden vein wriggles out of sight and reach so that it cannot be followed from the original opening in the earth, tunnels must be driven to intercept it. Some of these tunnels can be driven horizontally, or nearly, from slopes in the earth's surface; they are called adits. At other times the earth can simply be lifted off, leaving a pit where the gold is dug up. Both kinds of mining were done in Minas Gerais, but digging was difficult and dangerous there because the rock generally was friable and apt to cave in.

Much of the gold recovered in Brazil was not the ruddy metal of myth but a dark, smoky variety which the miners called *ouro preto*, black gold. The color was due to the presence of certain chemicals. Gold comes in many hues.

Added to placer and underground mining was the hydraulic method, which was effective but ruinous to the land. Again it was nothing new; hydraulic mining was old even in the early days of mining in Spain. It depends on water power. The temporary damming of auriferous streams gave the workers a chance to dig in dried water-beds at their leisure, but a far more ruinous proceeding was to direct strong jets of water on the land until the dirt was washed away into receptacles where it was panned or subjected to *cradling*—rocked or jigged up and down to help heavy sediments settle and light ones rise. There was never any attempt to replace the shifted earth; once it had been examined and the rock beneath denuded, the miners would go away to search other spots. Whole mountains have disappeared under hungry hydraulic mining, mountains in Spain and in the western United States as well as Brazil. What is left is usually pure desert. Climbing over the rusty, glaring hummocks of Ouro Preto in Minas Gerais, I have coughed in the arid dust and wiped my eyes so that I could see the old adits, their ruined openings dark in the sun shining down on despoiled country two and a half centuries later.

The prospectors and miners worked in very difficult conditions. For one thing, it took about twenty days to reach the diggings from São Paulo, but people were not put off by that, or by the fact that supplies were scarce when they got there. By 1697 there had appeared a string of encampments, villages, and mines all along the foot of the mountain range, where new gold discoveries were made almost daily, and people were happily confident that the land would not be worked out for many weeks to come. C. R. Boxer wrote that

no proper control was exercised over these people when they reached the mining area. They lived in anarchic conditions, and obeyed only the local rules that had been evolved to settle the conflicting claims to ground in the gold diggings and river beds. Crimes went unpunished, save by private vengeance, and murders and thefts abounded. . . .

Moreover, many of the miners were itinerant, being frequently on the move in search of new and richer strikes.

As is usual in such conditions, the miners were a motley crowd; to quote one observer, they were made up of "all sorts and conditions of persons: men and women; young and old; poor and rich; nobles and commoners; laymen, clergy, and religious of different orders."

The authorities were not happy about the gold discoveries. Little permanent good ever came of such wealth, they felt, and the people the mines attracted were not the sort to make desirable Brazilian settlers. What the country needed was fewer adventurers and more agriculturalists. What benefit in the end had Spain's incredibly rich gold and silver prizes proved at home? It would have been better for the nation not to have found the metals, and the same statement applied to Portugal, they said. But it was too late: The gold had been found, and all the government could do was attempt—vainly, in most cases—to prevent the wholesale desertion of African field hands from tobacco plantations and sugar mills to follow the uncertain fortunes of mining. The officials tried also, without dazzling success, to collect the so-called royal fifth, or tax, on what was dug up from the earth. One method attempted was to police the roads inland, but the gold seekers easily learned to evade such measures by taking to the bush when it was found prudent.

Strange side effects of the gold rush were many. Perhaps the chief anomaly was that the slave trade received a tremendous boost, English and Dutch slave traders along the coast of Guinea profiting from the high prices paid by gold miners in Brazil. It was observed that Africans worked harder and to better effect than their masters in the goldfields, though in that lawless country they found more opportunities to escape; many more had to be imported. Another difficulty in working the Brazilian mines was the shortage of food in the interior. The eager gold seekers were neither practical nor patient enough to plant their own supplies, so that the cost of food went up and up as imported provisions dwindled. More than one man (or woman, or child) died of starvation at such times, and the governor of Rio wrote to the crown in May 1698 that the food shortage "was so critical that most of the miners had been forced to abandon their dig-gings, and were wandering with their slaves in the woods, look-ing for game, fish, or fruits to eat." After a few years, however, the famine abated, partly because people began to be more sensi-ble and started small farms in the vicinity. They grew corn, potatoes, pumpkins, and beans; they raised pigs and chickens. Some of them found it paid better to supply food to the miners than to look for gold themselves. Later they even managed to raise cattle. All these foods, of course, sold for phenomenal prices.

How were the claims managed? These rules were laid down and observed long before the miners had time to turn their attention to more boring matters like laws against theft and mur-der. In theory the mining allotments, called *datas*, were dis-tributed fairly, but in practice it didn't work that way. The first man to discover gold in a new locality was given the right to choose the first two *datas* for himself. Two others were chosen next to them, the third for the Crown and the fourth for the Crown's representative. The rest of the claims were distributed by drawing lots. They were not of equal proportion but were measured according to how many slaves a man owned and worked. The *data* belonging to the Crown was then auctioned off, the money paid for it going into the Crown's exchequer. Once all this was settled the owners of *datas* were free to do what they wanted with them, buy or sell or exchange or amalgamate.

Naturally there was an immense amount of smuggling, in spite of all that appointed officials could do to collect the hated royal fifth, and like gold miners everywhere the men on the spot were incredibly extravagant with their booty, spending, gambling, and showing off generally. The most powerful among them had their own private armies to assist them in their careers. Furthermore, there were many complaints from the governors of Rio and Bahia that friars and clergymen had joined in the scramble, forgetting their vows and tempted by glitter to sacrifice their souls like all the others. In fact, they were the worst of the lot when it came to smuggling and nonpayment of dues to the Crown. It was easier for them than for laymen, said the complainants, because they could use sacred images for smuggling, hollowing out wooden figures and filling them with gold dust. Incidentally, the greatest fortunes were not made from gold itself: The richest man in

Minas Gerais won his wealth from "a judicious combination of mining, farming, slave trading, and merchandising," according to C. R. Boxer.

Soon the gloomy prophecies of the officials in Portugal and their representatives in Brazil were fulfilled: The gold rush proved nearly disastrous for the economy all over the empire. Merchants sent whatever they could in the way of foodstuffs, slaves, and commodities in general to the highest paying market, which was Minas Gerais. As a result, the prices of all these things shot up at home as well as at the gold mines. Workmen and craftsmen of all sorts followed the fashion and made for the mines, and even those who stayed at home charged what were described as outrageous prices for their labor. "Everywhere it was the same or a similar story," wrote Boxer.

In Bahia the immigrants from Portugal who normally filled the posts of overseers, bookkeepers, and cattle rangers were leaving en masse for the mines. New arrivals who were hired scarcely worked longer than the time necessary to earn the purchase price of a horse or some other means which would enable them to leave for the gold fields. . . . Worst of all, as Antonil [a Jesuit observer] wrote . . . : "the greatest part of the gold which is extracted from the mines is carried in gold dust and in coins to foreign kingdoms. The lesser part is that which remains in Portugal and in the cities of Brazil—save what is spent in braids, ornaments, and other fripperies with which the women of ill-fame and the Negresses are plentifully adorned nowadays, much more so than their lady owners."

Things went slowly in those days of sailing ships, and Lisbon learned very late that the Crown was not getting anything like its legal share of Brazilian gold. At the beginning, the collection of the royal fifths was taken care of, theoretically, at four smelting houses in the São Paulo region; smelting was forbidden for any-one but these accredited officials. But it was ingenuous to suppose that these places would suffice for all collections. Only one smelt-ing house was situated anywhere near the mines, and the mod-ern reader is struck by how much depended on the honor system: The miners were expected, or at least instructed, to bring their gold dust or nuggets, or both, in person to a smelting house, have it weighed out, watch the royal fifth removed (a painful process even to the most legally inclined), and see the rest of it cast into gold bars before it was given back. This was a lot to expect of human nature, and the miners were not usually the most righteous of persons to begin with. Besides, merely getting to a smelting house usually entailed a long, difficult journey which offered the gold's owners plenty of time for meditation. Small wonder that most of them found that they could make more advantageous arrangements. Like later-day miners in California and the Klondike, a man was accustomed to spend his gold dust, which he used as we use money, before he reached a smelting house rather than after. The interim also offered him a good chance to think of some way to get around the smelting house altogether, without official interference.

These smelting houses, explains Boxer, were not mints. It was against the law for anyone to melt down gold anywhere but in Portugal, where it was paid for in coin. But there were plenty of goldsmiths at the Brazilian mines, and they were willing to do the job for pay. Finally, in 1694, one mint was opened at Bahia with the government's blessing, to strike provincial coinage. It was moved five years later to Rio de Janeiro and was transferred again a year later to Pernambuco. The governor of Rio and the city council were not satisfied with this rather makeshift arrangement and urged that a proper mint be set up in that city, where, they hoped, it would be easier to collect the royal fifths and also make a profit out of seigniorage and brassage—the value of the coin over and above the costs of the bullion and minting. This was done at last in 1702, and a smelting house was included for those who wanted their gold in bars rather than coin. It was a good move as far as seigniorage and brassage was concerned; they made a large profit on those. But the royal fifths remained very hard to collect, even at Rio. To deal with this stubborn problem the governor of Rio, Artur de Sá, set up inspection stations on all the important trails leading out of the mines and made regulations by which nobody could get out of the region without a receipt to show how much gold he was carrying, what smelting house he was bound for, and where he intended to pay his royal fifths. It didn't work. Nothing worked. Reports Boxer:

As will be seen . . . these measures met with relatively little success, the yield from the fifths being particularly disappointing. From another source we learn that there were only thirty-six persons who paid the fifths in Minas Gerais in 1701, these contributors including a woman, a priest, and a friar. Only one such payment is recorded in 1702, and though there were eleven next year (including one of 504 drams), not until 1710 did the number of contributors to the fifths reach more than three figures.

A dram was a drachma, then valued at one eighth of an ounce. It did not take much common sense to realize that something was very wrong with Portuguese methods of taxation, especially as other sources of income from the New World showed up in the records as being far more profitable than gold, in spite of well-authenticated rumors of fortunes being made and spent by the miners. The authorities took further steps to get their money in 1704 by closing down the already existing smelting houses and moving them to two small seaports, hoping to capture the elusive fifths in this way, but it was no use. And all the time, gold in large amounts was flowing out of the country by other channels. It is impossible, says Boxer, to state exactly how much, as the sources are not dependable:

The latest writer on the subject shows that a steady increase in this gold [received in Lisbon] was recorded during the first decade of the eighteenth century. From 725 kilograms in 1699, it rose to 1,785 kilograms two years later, and to 4,350 kilograms in 1703. This rise continued until the impressive total of 14,500 kilograms was reached in 1712. In addition there was a parallel stream of contraband gold imported.

There were three other gold rushes in Brazil: at Cuiabá, in the west, in 1718; at Goiás in 1725; and at Guaporé in the Mato Grosso in 1734. Cuiabá is a river, and a rich lode of placer gold was found there, with the same result as at Minas Gerais: people dropping their daily tasks to hurry to the mines, leaving behind them a deserted countryside and a grave problem of missing manpower. The main difference was that to reach Cuiabá and the diggings entailed a journey of seven months by canoe on strange waterways through Indian country. Many died of disease on the way or after they got there. Collection of the royal fifths was no easier than it had been in Minas Gerais.

In an article published in August 1969 in *The Hispanic American Historical Review,* C. R. Boxer goes into more detail about those later years. The situation regarding the outflow of gold had not changed, at least not for the better. In 1715 there was an attempt on the part of the Portuguese government to ban English factors—men of international trade, merchants and the like —from their colonial cities, especially those in Brazil, because they made more profit than the Portuguese themselves. The argument went on for years, without either side making very definite gains. What did not change was that contraband gold passed through British hands at the Brazilian ports without interruption.

Serious as was the contraband gold trade at Brazilian ports, particularly Bahia and Rio de Janeiro [wrote Boxer], it did not annoy the Portuguese government quite so much as did the continual drain of Brazilian gold from Lisbon to England, since the former involved chiefly gold-dust, the latter gold coins. . . . [T]he balance of trade was heavily in England's favor, as Consul Burnett reminded his government in September 1721: "For as the British manufactures imported for the consumption of this kingdom and of its colonies amount to more than five times the value of all the commodities exported from hence, it is evident that the overplus must be remitted in specie."

Another British diplomat, Baron Tyrawly, British envoy in Lisbon, wrote in 1732:

The penalty of running gold is very great . . . and the temptation to it is also very considerable. . . . The traders to the Mines, finding this duty too heavy upon them, have chosen for several years to run the risk, which they have hitherto done with great success; and the gold they brought in this clandestine way, whether in dust or in bar, has been bought chiefly by our English Factors, from whence our own Mint in the Tower has been from time to time so well supplied.

Most Brazilian gold remitted to or via England from Lisbon was sent either by the weekly Falmouth packet boats or by Royal Navy ships, all of them immune from search by the Portuguese customs. The gold was brought from the Lisbon waterfront to the ships in boats, the crews of which were heavily armed with cutlasses, swords, and pistols, though it was considered in good taste to keep the weapons out of sight. There were many fights, however, between Portuguese longshoremen and English sailors along the waterfront, leading to numerous complaints, and King

John V, who could see the fights from his palace windows, didn't
like the view at all. Tyrawly wrote on this subject on September
29, 1734, to the Duke of Newcastle. Boxer explains that His
Lordship was not a typical diplomat but "an irascible Irishman
who had served with distinction" in battle during the War of the
Spanish Succession and was badly wounded at Malplaquet. He
"affected a soldierly bluffness, so that his dispatches are . . . com-
pulsively quotable," as in this passage:

Your Grace may be assured, the King of Portugal would not care, or
complain, how often a parcel of drunken English seamen and Portuguese porters and watermen beat one another, if there was not a
circumstance that His Majesty lays more to heart. Your Grace perhaps
does not know, that there is not an English man of war homeward-
bound from almost any point of the compass, that does not take Lisbon
in their way home, and more especially if it be at a time when the
Portuguese Rio de Janeiro and Bahia Fleets are expected. The reason
of this is in hopes that when the effects of these Fleets are given out,
that they may pick up some freight by carrying part of it to England.
This, I know, My Lord, puts the King of Portugal out of all patience,
because it is breaking in so plain and barefaced a manner upon the
prohibition of carrying money and gold-dust out of his country. Indeed,
if there was no other method for us to send it home, this would be right,
but we have our packets that go constantly and merchant-men that
usually attend the Lisbon trades, that are fully sufficient to carry our
balance home. And both these have their plausible pretence of coming
here, the packets with our letters, the merchant-men with our goods;
besides that the officers and even the sailors of these are so acquainted
with the nature of the place that they know how to go about this
business privately and discreetly. But everybody knows that a man of
war can have no other business in life here but to carry away money;
and they generally go about it so awkwardly, that I have often wondered they are not caught in the fact. The ships of the Newfoundland
station constantly touch here on their way home, how many leagues it
is out of their way I need not tell your Grace.

The same correspondent had written to Newcastle on May 30,
1728, "About four months since, one of the King's ships that was
here when the Brazil Fleet came in, carried to England 100,000
moedas, another carried 20,000 two months since, and during
the time I have been here all the King's ships that have gone from
hence, which are about four or five, have all carried away money,

more or less, and the packet-boats as regularly as they go out."
He added that the purser of H.M.S. *Winchester* personally had
carried several thousand moedas daily on board his ship between
July 21 and August 10, 1720, including "upwards of 6,000" on one
of those days alone. Captain Augustus Hervey, R.N., took home
a freight of 80,000 moedas from Lisbon in 1748 and another
63,533 moedas in 1753, apart from 30,000 moidores from Lisbon
to Gibraltar and Italy in 1752. Between March 25, 1740, and June
8, 1741, the Falmouth packets carried Brazilian gold to a total of
£447,347, and more in 1759 (£787,290) and 1760 (£1,085,559).
The Portuguese often threatened to stop and search the ship's
boats of the men-of-war and the packets, but they never did. If
they did, wrote Tyrawly in 1732, "there will be absolutely an end
of all remittances of gold-dust, bars, moedas, and diamonds to
England, and consequently of the balance of trade."

Tyrawly criticized the Royal Navy captains for indulging in the
contraband trade and Lisbon factory merchants for being indiscreet. Once, when his government instructed him to demand the
return of some 175 moedas which Portuguese customs officers
had confiscated from a British merchantship, he replied, on April
17, 1734:

It is impossible for Your Grace to conceive the indiscretion of people
here in that so dangerous article of their business, and the merchants
here will talk as publicly upon the Exchange of what money they have
shipped for England, and with as little secrecy send it on board, as they
do a chest of oranges. If people will be so indiscreet, they must take
their sufferings for the reward of their indiscretion.

It was his opinion, expressed in a private letter, that most of the
members of the Lisbon factory were "a parcel of the greatest
jackanapes I ever met with; Fops, Beaux, drunkards, gamesters,
and prodigiously ignorant, even in their own business."

The people in London, he felt, were equally indiscreet. When
large consignments of Brazilian gold arrived by ship in London,
that city's newspapers regularly announced the fact: "It is a most
miserable thing," he wrote,

that there is no stopping the mouths of our news writers; they set down
the gold they hear, or dream, we extract from Portugal with just as little
caution, as they do the oats and barley that are sold at Bear Key. . . .

If these people could be confined to the accounts of highwaymen, and horses stolen or strayed, their papers would be every bit as diverting and instructive to the generality of their readers.

Boxer comments that this is no new complaint. Lord Tyrawly wrote that letter in 1738, but one of his predecessors at Lisbon had written home in March 1716:

One thing I must desire you would be so kind as to mention to Mr. Stanhope, that we find it extremely inconvenient that the writers of our newspapers should be suffered to insert (as they have done of late) that the men of war and packet-boats from hence import vast sums of gold, —as for example the *Gibraltar* man of war that went late from hence, our papers say she carried £200,000 sterling in gold (which is about ten times as much as she really had on board). This was immediately transcribed into the Portuguese *Gazette* printed in this city, with a malicious design (I don't doubt) of enraging the populace against us that are livers [residents] here, who were already too much our enemies on account of the jealousy they entertained of our merchants carrying off their bullion; and now they see it confirmed in our own as well as in their prints [they] are ready to rise against us. For though the government here have been all along sensible that the exportation of their gold has been and must be unavoidable (they having nothing else wherewith to balance our trade), yet the commonalty have in great measure been kept ignorant of it, and reckon it a heinous crime in us to rob them (as they call it) in such a manner.

The country around Ouro Preto in Minas Gerais looks like Arizona, except that Arizona doesn't have so many sharp little hills and scooped-out hollows. There is little verdure. A few cattle roam around, looking for mouthfuls of food. Everywhere, even near the museum, a smell pervades that reminded me of my own Midwest on a hot day—clay or sand baking in the sun. It was altogether a reddish-yellow landscape, and though I tried hard I could not repopulate it in my mind with those hustling, bustling seekers after gold. But then all that was a long time ago.

8

"WHAT COINS?"

The stretch of sand that runs along for miles at the margin of
Cape Canaveral was irresistibly reminiscent, I thought, of Cape
Cod. But then one sandspit is very like another, except for the
temperature surrounding it. That day the sea was remarkably
peaceful though not very blue; it reflected a gunmetal sky. Here
and there a family party sat on the sand and ate, but the place
was by no means crowded, if you didn't count the sea gulls, and
nobody seemed eager to go into the water. It was not easy to
believe that this dull, peaceful surface covered, possibly, any
number of decaying broken spars, old bones, and silver and gold
coins. But it does—perhaps. On a shallow sea bottom like that one
never knows, and nothing stays the same underwater, though I
always thought it did until I read Kip Wagner's book, *Pieces of
Eight.*

Wagner was a builder. Not a metallurgist, not an adventurer,
not a geologist, but a building contractor from Ohio who moved
to Florida because he liked it. He and his family lived in a hamlet
called Wabasso, about 120 miles north of Miami, near a larger
town called Sebastian on the Sebastian Inlet and not far from
Cape Canaveral (or Cape Kennedy, depending on your preference). Cape Whichever not much later was to be the home of
space experiments. (The first sky shot was in 1950.) One of Wagner's temporary partners on a job mentioned one day in 1949
that it would be a good time to go out looking for coins on the
sand. They were taking shelter after a brief but busy storm,
during which breakers had pounded the beach.

"What coins?" asked Wagner, and the other man, hardly able

to credit such ignorance, explained. Every so often after a storm, he said, the sea cast up on the beach strangely shaped pieces of metal that were, in spite of their dark appearance, made of genuine silver and came from old Spanish wrecks. They were, in fact, the legendary "pieces of eight" mentioned so often in *Treasure Island* and got their name from the fact that they had been worth eight reals (a Spanish monetary unit) apiece. Their strange shape was due to the way they were made: not minted piece by piece, but cut off a silver bar and then stamped. Naturally they were so irregular that no two pieces were alike.

Fascinated, Wagner began looking on his own for these coins whenever he had a chance to stroll on the beach. He talked to friends and neighbors and heard a number of mouth-watering stories, learning that lucky people might even find gold coins among the silver. The village was full of treasure lore. One man, it was said, had built into his fireplace an extremely heavy brick he found near the sea, and the brick melted the first time he built a fire. It must have been gold, the legend went, or at least silver. Wagner saw his first genuine piece of eight when a drunken assistant took him to the beach and showed where he had accumulated a cache of seven of the things, black and roughly rectangular. So that's what they looked like! Wagner realized that he had probably seen them before many times, but had dismissed them as worthless fragments because the sulfated silver was black, not bright and glittering as one would expect. Though he didn't yet realize it, he was captivated, hooked, by the thought of treasure seeking.

The same partner who had introduced him to the subject of castaway coins now took him further by suggesting that they investigate a wreck that had become visible off the beach; Wagner learned to call it a "wreck site." It was not far off, three miles south of Sebastian Inlet and lying in a mere four or five feet of water—very tempting to a treasure seeker. With four companions Kip Wagner devoted most of that summer to the investigation of the wreck. They lived in the open air, slept in hammocks, and wore bathing suits most of the time. Pooling their money, they rented the necessary equipment. The wreck was only seventy-five to one hundred feet from shore, but even so it was too far away for a dragline, as the guide rope is called. They would therefore bulldoze mounds of sand on the beach and, when the tide went out, push the sand into the water, building a kind of temporary pier from which they would run their dragline out to the wreck. Later, when the tide came in and washed away the sand pier, it simply meant that they would have to build it up again at the next opportunity. Whenever possible the dragline operator scooped up shovelfuls of sand and dumped it on the beach, where his partners were waiting with metal detectors to look through it. It was a very primitive operation that led to nothing except ruined pieces of a long-sunk ship, but it was good practice. Later the treasure seekers found that their so-called wreck was, in fact, merely a piece of a ship, the rest of which was probably far away under the waves; the waters where they were working were far too shallow in any case to have been host to a Spanish galleon. At the end of the summer they had spent all their money, some $12,000, and had nothing but experience to show for it—that and, for Kip Wagner, at least, a deep-seated determination to carry on. He did not realize it himself; the fruitless summer had left him tired and ashamed for having put his family at risk. All he had found for his pains was one coin, his first, a Spanish copper dated 1649 called a *maravedi*. He valued it so little that he gave it to one of the partners.

But with spring and summer the old fascination returned. One day he went out with a metal detector, determined to find at least one piece of eight, until at last his stubbornness was rewarded. After that he found more; once, after "a lively northeaster," he picked up five of them. Some of the coins were not pieces of eight, but gold. After a time he had amassed thirty-five or forty gold coins, carefully stowed away in his wife's chest because he was not sure whether he was permitted to keep them: He was so ignorant of the subject that he had never heard of treasure trove, the law that applies to finders. (It is not always a question of "finders, keepers," but nowadays one does keep some, at least, of one's discoveries.) The silver coins, however, Wagner gave away or made of them crude jewelry for children. Where did they come from? Why did they escape his eyes one day and pop up in the same place on the next? Wagner had an idea that the storms probably loosened and washed out the earth of the bluffs in which they were hidden, and that waves kept them from drifting out to sea, but after a while he changed his mind. Noticing that most of the coins were found at the foot of the bluffs after storms, he was forced to believe that they were washed ashore whenever the wind was high. Yes, there must be a source out there under the water. With a friend he tried some primitive snorkeling, but never got a coin from that.

Dr. Kelso, another friend of his who was also called Kip, refused to believe this theory. The coins had been there all the time, he argued, buried in the sand, and that was why they showed up after storms. The sand on top of the treasure simply washed out to sea in rough weather. Kip Kelso was director of the Health Department, a man of education who shared Wagner's interest in the coins and their origin. The men first discovered their mutual interest when Kelso dropped in one evening to give Wagner a physical examination for an insurance policy and found the Wagner couple kneeling on the floor, studying maps of the East Coast. Kelso knew more than a little about the history of the state and the Spanish fleets that had once sailed Florida's seas. He proved to be a stimulating and encouraging friend, and they had many discussions on the subject of wrecked treasure. It was during such a conversation that Wagner mentioned a peculiar fact he had noticed: Not one of the coins he had found carried a mint date later than 1715. It was an odd little observation to be filed away for future reference.

One day after a particularly ruinous storm, Wagner was the first person to go down to the beach. He found everything so stirred up it was almost unrecognizable, but he made one important discovery—a bright piece of silver dated 1714 which differed from any he had yet found. Surely it had been washed ashore just the night before from a wreck! Dr. Kelso refused to admit the significance of the find. It too, he said, had been buried on shore, undoubtedly; all they had to do was dig up a portion of the beach and Wagner would find that he was right, because there would be innumerable coins under the sand. The argument waxed hot. To prove his point, Kelso rented a ditchdigger, and the men dug three trenches seventy-five feet long and several feet deep, which crisscrossed each other so that no important part of the beach was left unturned. They found no coins. Dr. Kelso now admitted that he might have been mistaken and that there was only one other explanation: The coins were indeed washed ashore from some hidden cache underwater. But what could it be? The answer, thought Kip Wagner, must lie in Spanish history, and he set to work to find out what had happened in 1715 or after—but not too long after.

It did not take long to learn of a flotilla, or *flota,* to use the Spanish word, wrecked (according to local lore) in a hurricane off Cape Canaveral in 1715. There had been some survivors of the disaster, and a good deal was known about it. The sailing of the flotilla was an annual event; it was known as the Silver Fleet, or Plate Flota, for obvious reasons, and the 1715 ships were supposed to be carrying a cargo of treasure worth $14 million in gold, silver, and jewels (emeralds and diamonds) when it was wrecked—at Cape Canaveral, according to the legend—but Wagner soon ran into confusion on this point. He sent his shiny silver 1714 coin to the Smithsonian Institution in Washington, D.C., with a letter asking if it could possibly have come from the 1715 flotilla that sank off Cape Canaveral. He addressed this letter quite properly to the curator of Armed Forces history, a man named Mendel Peterson, who replied that the silver coin could not possibly be from the Silver Fleet because that flotilla had been wrecked not at Canaveral but two hundred miles away, off the Florida Keys. Peterson was very downright about it, and poor Kip Wagner was downcast, not to say confused. How could there have been two Silver Fleets wrecked in one year? There couldn't. Yet how could the locals be so mistaken? Clearly more research was indicated.

Aided by Dr. Kelso, the untrained Wagner got to work on all the books in all the available libraries, looking for the Silver Fleet. The task was enormous because of the great number of ship-wrecks for which the Florida coast was notorious. How to sort them out? It was a task that had to be done, and the friends worked for a long time before they had a stroke of luck. Or perhaps it is unfair to call it luck; Dr. Kelso was a persistent researcher, and he found the clue. On a motoring vacation, Dr. Kelso's family camped in their trailer near Washington, D.C., while he looked into what might be pertinent to the subject in the Library of Congress. In a book called *Armada Española* by Césario Fernandez Duro, published in 1900, he found a good deal about the Silver Fleet of 1715. Then he looked carefully through an article written by a Yale professor, Irving Rouse, about Spanish fleets. Here he hit on one of the professor's references, a work by an English cartographer named Bernard Romans, published in 1775. If Professor Rouse had found it useful, reasoned Kelso, there was possibly something about Wagner's lost fleet in it. He tried to find it, but was first told that they didn't have it in the library. After a careful search, however, the librarians did find a copy of the work in the rare book section.

Dr. Kelso found in this volume far more than he had dared to hope. There it was, written out:

Directly opposite the south of the St. Sebastians River happened the shipwreck of the Spanish Admiral, who was the northernmost wreck of fourteen galleons, and a hired Dutch ship, all laden with specie and plate; which by (action) of northeast winds were drove ashore and lost on this coast, between this place and the bleach-yard, in 1715. A hired Frenchman fortunately escaped, by having steered half a point more east than the others. . . . The people employed in the course of our survey, while walking the strand after strong eastern gales, have repeatedly found pistareens and double pistareens, which kinds of money probably yet remaining in the wrecks, are sometimes washed up by the surf in hard winds. This lagoon stretches parallel to the sea, until the latitude 27:20, where it has an outwatering, or mouth; directly before this mouth, in three fathom water, lie the remains of the Dutch wreck. The banks of this lagoon are not fruitful.

A map accompanied this passage, and when Kelso looked at it all doubt vanished. There was the San Sebastian River, there was Cape Canaveral, and there was *not* Sebastian Inlet, because it didn't exist at that time. (Sandspits are apt to change.) A note said, "Opposite this River, perished the Admiral, commanding the Plate Fleet 1715, the rest of the fleet 14 in number, between this and ye Bleech Yard."

"The River," said Wagner, had to be the Sebastian Creek, as it is now known. There could be little doubt now in the minds of Kelso and Wagner: Their wrecked fleet was there, not off the Keys or Cape Canaveral or anywhere else. An added notation, "el Palmar," was explained without difficulty later on, when they were able to study the Romans account more closely. One of the galleons had tried to get into the shelter of a lagoon called the

Indian River through an inlet on a point seven leagues from the Palmar de Ais, the palm grove of the Ais Indians who used to live there.

To double-check, Dr. Kelso went on to New York and had an interview with the president of the American Numismatic Society, Henry Gruenthall. He was armed with a number of photographs of the coins he and Wagner had found. Gruenthall, impressed by the pictures, was excited and enthusiastic. He made various helpful suggestions, and Kelso moved on to the Spanish-American Association of New York, where people were equally helpful, referring him to librarians in Havana and Mexico City. Kelso and Wagner wrote to these people, but here they struck a snag: Neither the Cubans nor the Mexicans seemed inclined to help them. Were they suspicious of North Americans on principle? Well, then, what about Spain? Wagner had heard that the General Archives of the Indies, in Seville, was full of information. He obtained the name of the curator and wrote to him, first taking the trouble to have his letter translated into Spanish. But the reply, when at last it arrived, was disappointing: Dr. Don José de la Peña was guarded, telling the Americans nothing they did not already know.

The treasure seekers were not to be discouraged. A friend of theirs, a woman they knew well, was about to visit Spain, and they commissioned her to visit Dr. Peña in person, show him some pieces of eight, and find out what the trouble was. Much to her surprise, when she spoke to the archivist face to face and showed him the coins he burst into tears, explaining that he had simply not been allowed to answer questions about the fleet: His superiors thought they smelled a rat. Most likely they had hoped somehow to grab the treasure for themselves. After all, back in 1715 it *had* been Spanish, and one feels that their claims, if any, had some justification. But there was no immediate possibility of their defying the United States and entering Florida waters, and Dr. Peña assured his visitor that though he was forbidden to answer her questions directly, after she left Spain he would mail to her copies of the relevant papers. She returned empty-handed but hopeful, sure, she said, that the doctor would carry out his promise. And so he did: Within a few days a package containing 3,000 feet of microfilm arrived from the archives in Seville.

Even now their problems were not settled. The microfilm contained a large number of manuscripts, letters, and the like, but
they were written in archaic Spanish, with a number of words
spelled phonetically, as they had been in the eighteenth century.
All the following year Dr. Kelso and Kip Wagner worked on their
prize, until, as Wagner put it, pieces of the puzzle began to fall
into place. They learned a lot about those seventeenth-century
and eighteenth-century silver fleets. They learned their names,
what cargo they carried, and the names of captains and crews.
They were delighted to learn from this reading that less than half
of the fleet's treasure had been brought up: it was supposed, in
all, to be worth $14 million worth of gold, silver and jewelry.

Part of what the treasure seekers learned was that at the time
of the storm off Sebastian, flotillas like the wrecked one were an
old story. For more than two hundred years, at the cost of nobody
knows how much death and cruelty, these ships had sailed from
the New World to the Old, laden with treasure for the Spanish
crown. None of this was a secret from the other nations of
Europe, which for a long time had been trying, often with success, to make battle with the leaders of the fleets in order to take
these famous galleons as prizes. Sir Walter Raleigh's whole life
and success were built around his feats of piracy, as were those
of other desperadoes of the time. In reaction, the armadas were
built stronger each year. "The Bureau of Trade and the Council
of the Indies laid down strict rules for fleet admirals to follow,"
wrote Wagner, speaking of official Spanish bodies. "Treasure-
bearing cargo ships were to cross the Atlantic in convoys of six
to 10, each escorted by heavier galleons and lighter, utility vessels, which served as scouts for the fleets." By the middle of the
sixteenth century the arrangements had settled to a pattern: Two
armadas were to go every year to the Indies. Consisting of merchant vessels and their escorts, armed warships, they were called
the Nueva España and the Tierra Firma flotillas. On the trip west
they carried supplies for the colonies: clothing, provisions (including wines), glassware, ironware, and mining equipment;
coming back they were loaded, as we know, with treasure. They
had two different routes: The Nueva España fleet sailed for Vera-
cruz by way of Puerto Rico, Hispaniola, and Cuba; the Tierra
Firma ships traveled via Venezuela. Coming back they com-

bined in Havana, then sailed through the Florida Straits and along the New Bahamas Channel, turning to the east between St. Augustine and Cape Hatteras. It was a dangerous voyage but the best that could be worked out. Usually the commanders tried to set out in June before the storms got a good start.

Each armada was led by the *capitana,* a large fighting galleon, heavily armed, which carried treasure but no other cargo. Behind the fleet came a second armed galleon called the *almirante* —in other words, the captain and the admiral. Both ships carried lots of cannon. Each *capitana* carried the general—that is, the commanding officer of the fleet—and on each *almirante* was, as seems fitting, an admiral. He assumed command of the armada in case of pirate attacks. If it seems strange that a general should have accompanied each fleet as a matter of course, well, that was Spanish custom. They had no naval captains; generals took their place. There were various classes of cargo ships in the armada. The *nao,* like a galleon but with more freight capacity, was the chief kind of transport vessel. Rather like *naos* but with less cargo space were the *urcas. Galleoncetes,* light and speedy, were the scouts. Escort vessels called *navios* were warships—floating forts, Wagner called them.

Of course, out of all the wealth that the ships carried, the Spanish kings and courts claimed their royal fifth, which was as much a grievance to the merchants as the income tax is to us today. To avoid as much of the tax as possible, the alert traders who imported treasure from Spanish America did their best to undervalue the cargoes they sent, bribing the shipping officials to back them up. It was expensive to bribe, but not so expensive as paying the true tax would have been, and practically everybody did it. The 1715 armada, as it happens, was unusually heavily laden with treasure, since there had been no regular sailings for the previous thirteen years owing to the War of the Spanish Succession. Unfortunately, both sections of the combined fleet were unusually slow in getting started, and even after they met there was more delay in Havana. A French ship, *El Grifón,* had received permission to sail with the flota—ships often did this in the interests of safety from pirates—and it, too, was responsible for more waiting. In fact, it was July 14, long after the safest season, before the armada at last got under way past El Morro.

At least it was a beautiful day, with no hint of trouble in the offing, but that is the way with Caribbean weather—it can change very quickly.

The ships, with two thousand men aboard, were a handsome sight—"more eye-catching, however, than practical," to quote Kip Wagner, because Spanish ships were much less manageable and more difficult to maneuver than their English opposite numbers, sleeker and lighter as they were. Still, it was a lovely sight as they sailed across the Florida Straits and then among the Florida Keys.

The first hint of trouble came on Monday, July 29, when seasoned sailors looked with misgivings at a haze in the sky. Parallel to the fleet but several hundred miles to the east a hurricane was boiling up, and on Monday evening it changed direction and headed west, as if deliberately to intercept the flota. Tuesday morning the weather around the ships was ominously even— dead calm interspersed with sudden winds, and wisps of clouds which in the course of time became heavy. By Tuesday afternoon it was so dark that the ships' lanterns were lit. The waves had grown large, and the sailors were battening down the hatches.

It was too late to seek shelter in any cove, as Wagner said, reliving the storm. The fleet was still near Cape Canaveral, and the leading generals knew that the coastline as far as Canaveral was full of natural ship-wrecking hazards: shoals and reefs. They had to meet the storm head-on.

They went, then, through the progressive stages of the hurricane—squalls repeating with mounting fury, and wind and rain battering the ships through the early half of the night, until 2 A.M., when the full hurricane was unleashed. Winds of 100 miles per hour cracked masts and tore loose the secured sails, ripping them into ribbons. Seamen were swept from the decks to be lost in the swirling seas. Each captain tried desperately to maneuver his ship, but the galleons were driven, slowly and inexorably, toward shore. When they struck at last, some men were thrown straight into the boiling sea; others tried for a while to paddle. There were shattered beams falling everywhere. One by one the ships were hurled to destruction. Not all the men were lost, though both generals were.

One ship got away. This was the French *El Grifón,* whose

captain, Daré, kept her clear of the reefs by disobeying orders from on high and sailing a half point farther northeast than the others. It was thanks to this ship's crew and their knowledgeable observations that history knows just what happened to the Plate Fleet of 1715, for though there were about a thousand survivors, most of them were too stunned, hungry, and generally fatigued to know what had happened to them; they just lay on the sand and slowly recovered.

Looking around the beach as it is today, peaceful with its family picnics and probably a quite different shape, I found it hard to envisage what it must have been like that long-ago morning after the storm cleared away. The survivors soon became aware of their needs: They had to have food and water if not immediate shelter. The nearest place where these things were to be found was St. Augustine, a good way to the north. Fortunately at least one longboat had outlasted the storm and was there, close in to the beach. Some of the strongest men were told to sail this boat to St. Augustine, carry the news of the wreck, and bring help, while the others waited on the deserted sands.

Typically, some of these men were not so badly off that they could forget the fascination of the treasure. Indeed, they were not permitted to forget it, because all around them on the beach lay scattered parts of it, coins and jewels of a value none of them had ever seen before. Gold and silver twinkled in the sun. Distracted from thoughts of hunger and cold and their generally hard fate, they grabbed baubles and coins, hid them in their tattered clothing, and looked around for somewhere to conceal themselves with their loot. Others paid no attention. In the meantime the boatload of hardier survivors finally reached St. Augustine, after a combination of sailing and trudging that lasted several days; there they told their story and said that a thousand men at Sebastian were dying for lack of food and drink. A rescue party was quickly organized by the Spanish colonists and sent to the aid of the survivors, but the rescuers, like the deserters, were not so distressed by the human side of the story that they forgot the most important part of it, the treasure cargo of the lost ships. At the same time that they gathered people to help save the sufferers, they notified the proper authorities and told them of the looting. A band of soldiers was immediately sent to Matanzas

Inlet, where people coming from the south along Florida's coast would have to cross, and there the soldiers waited for anyone trying to sneak off with gold, silver, and jewels. To reach St. Augustine was the deserters' only hope; it was the one gateway to the mainland of Florida. Sure enough, after a fairly long wait the soldiers spied the first deserter, and then another, and then another. Loaded down with heavy precious metal they made their painful way to the stream, where it was easy for the guard to pick them up. Every single thief was caught; later they were executed, and the booty returned to its rightful owners. But much treasure, of course, still lay scattered on the sea floor among the battered ships that lay offshore.

To take charge of the salvage, Don Juan del Hoyo Solórzano was sent over from Havana in March 1716. He set up camp a couple of miles south of Sebastian Inlet and, with a number of Indian divers, got to work. First they had to find what was left of the dead ships; naturally, by this time there was a coating of sand over all, and even after this or that ship was located it was not easy to find what they wanted. One of del Hoyo's Indians would hold his breath, take hold of a heavy stone to carry him to the bottom, and jump in head foremost. Once there, for as long as he could hold his breath he looked around for treasure; then he came up to report. Some of them carried inverted buckets for an extra supply of air, but none of this work could be done except when the water was clear enough for them to see. It was said that a third of the Indian diving force died at the work. Once an Indian had spotted something that looked like treasure, he came up again to fetch a line which, with companions to help, he could tie to the thing. It was then hauled up. A good deal of treasure was thus recovered, and del Hoyo built a fort at his camp to keep it in. He also kept very careful records of what had been salvaged.

Soon they were in trouble from pirates who came to fish in their waters, "like sharks," as Kip Wagner said; sometimes more time was spent chasing off pirate ships than recovering treasure. The newcomers didn't always try to fish up prey from the waters; one, an English privateer commanded by a Captain Henry Jennings, who was legally committed to suppress piracy, went a step farther and robbed the Spaniards on land of the treasure they had so arduously rescued from the water. Jennings raided the base camp and got away with silver worth 350,000 pesos. After this incident the Spaniards reinforced their guards.

By the end of two years, del Hoyo thought he had taken off the cream of the treasure. What was left called for too much hard slogging, and in 1718 he leased off the work to a contractor, who got more out of the ocean bed and caught a lot more pirates in the process. It was almost four years before all operations on the Plate Fleet of 1715 were wound up. Wagner and Kelso calculated that Spain had recovered about $6 million worth of treasure, less than half of what went down. This was too bad for eighteenth-century Spain but very encouraging to the treasure seekers of the twentieth century, and Kip Wagner went about his search with a refreshed spirit. Now he had something more definite to look for on the beach: He wanted to find the remains, if any, of the campsite and fortress where Don Juan stacked up, however temporarily, the pieces of eight he got from the divers. Wagner bought a good metal detector and started working on the beach, back and forth in a methodical pattern.

At first he had no luck—no, what he had was *bad* luck. The detector showed him where to dig, over and over, and over and over he uncovered beer cans, bedsprings, and all kinds of other metallic trash. Days passed in such boring exercises, and he was getting more and more discouraged, when one day he found a depression in a large mound in the sand, a big depression, covered with growth. Obviously it had been there a long time. At its bottom water glittered, and an old dog that had taken to following him on his walks went over and lapped it. Lapped salt water? It was not possible, thought Wagner. He tasted the water himself —yes, it was sweet. This must be a man-made well, he reasoned; it might even be the one dug for the campsite he was looking for. That day of all days, however, he hadn't brought the detector. No matter; he ran home and got it, tested the well, and got a strong reaction. He dug, bringing up first a ship's spike, and next a cannonball. The metal detector was screaming excitedly. This was too big for him to tackle by himself, thought Kip Wagner. He measured out the liveliest area (according to the detector) and found that it covered half an acre. He went home and wrote to the secretary of the South Florida Historical Society, who answered the letter by appearing in person, bringing with him a geologist. They agreed that Wagner's half-acre must be the site of the old fort. It was gratifying, to say the least. Kip lost no time measuring out his claim and registering it. Interestingly enough, the historian and the geologist made no protest against Wagner's vandalizing an archaeological site. But then, gold can make people forget such matters.

Wagner rented a bulldozer and cleared the area of all scrub; then, with a shovel and screen, he began the long job of sifting through the surface soil, two feet deep. It was slow work, but almost never fruitless. There were Peruvian and Mexican potsherds. There were the hopper and shaft of a small coffee mill, fragments of olive jars, musket balls, a bullet mold, and sheets of lead. It all fitted into life as it must have been lived in a Spanish encampment. As the days went by, realizing that he could hardly do it all himself, Wagner hired a black man who helped with the digging. One day, a few inches beneath the surface, he found a pair of cutlasses, the blades nearly gone from rust. Soon after that find his detector led him to three black rough rectangles that turned out to be made of silver; he had dug up three pieces of eight that Jennings must have missed. As if this were not enough, the detector next led him to a golden artifact, a ring set with a diamond, the metal so soft and pure that the diamond was halfway down in the prongs. This was a large stone of 2.5 carats; set in the band were six tiny diamonds as well.

Because of his patients, Dr. Kelso couldn't come out to help very often, but Wagner kept him informed of the latest developments. Although Wagner had now furnished himself with a new and better detector, he was still working hard after four or five months of labor, so now and then he took a rest by breaking off and going for a swim in the surf not far from his campsite—just lazily paddling around, as he put it. He usually took with him on these expeditions his little son, who played on the beach while Daddy played in the water. Wagner had a homemade face mask for diving, and sometimes an old rubber tube. These things did well enough for hit-and-miss snorkeling, but he finally made a better toy, a surfboard with a hole cut in it at one end in which he fitted a pane of glass.

"Remember," he wrote, " . . . this was still before scuba equipment received . . . its . . . national popularity boom." He found it surprisingly effective. So much so, indeed, that one day as he was floating about looking down, he made an important (and very large) find: four or five ship's cannon each eight- or nine-feet long. They were in only eight or nine feet of water. He kept diving and poking around until he uncovered a huge anchor. "Without doubt this was a wreck site," he wrote, "the first I'd found." It made sense. The campsite had been constructed deliberately close to as many wrecks as possible. Thrilled, Wagner carefully marked the spot by clearing the shore with his bulldozer into a wide arrow pointing directly at the wreck in the water. Why had he taken so long to find it? Because, he explained, he hadn't known just what to look for. In his imagination, a wrecked Spanish galleon was just like a sailing galleon, with hull intact and masts erect, except that it would be lying on its side on the ocean floor. Actually, all the wood of the ship, or nearly all of it, would have vanished, eaten away by the teredo, or shipworm, years earlier; not only the wooden hull and masts would have vanished, but so would treasure chests and barrels made of the same material. A saltwater animal, the teredo spares wood only in places like the Baltic Sea where the water is too salty for it. What a treasure seeker should look for are cannon, anchors, and/or heaps of ballast stones.

For a time after that Kip Wagner thought he might cut things short by flying over the coast, where with any luck he could spot wrecks from on high. Though he spent a lot of money that way and a good deal of time, it didn't work. Not only did wood rot and disappear through the action of teredos, but the sea seemed determined to camouflage even metal with corrosion and coral deposits. Silver converts to silver sulfide, and iron oxidizes. Gold, of course, doesn't tarnish, no matter how long it lies underwater —or, as we know from Tutenkhamon's tomb, under earth. Brass cannon corrode, but not very much; they often turn green, however. Iron cannon may seem well preserved, but after they are brought up and exposed to air they can deteriorate. Masses of silver may acquire crusts of calcareous or sandy deposits, after which coral grows on them and completely disguises the original shapes. Porcelain remains intact, and often, surprisingly enough, so does steel.

"I have often seen paper," wrote Wagner, " . . . pages of an early Bible—in perfect condition after centuries under the sea. Figure that one out." He added that even a wreck site, complete with cannon and ballast, is not necessarily the remains of a treasure ship. There are many other dead ships on the ocean floor— warships and others. Just the same, he felt in his bones that this wreck, his first, was one of the 1715 treasure galleons, and he was excited. So was Doc Kip Kelso, who, to celebrate, bought his friend a complete diving outfit with flippers, regulator, and air tank.

9

GENUINE TREASURE

Wagner dived and dived. He found more cannon and, to whet his appetite, a small cluster of tiny silver coins fused into what was undoubtedly originally a leather pouch, the cover of which had long since disappeared. But if there was real treasure in this wreck, he would never be able to handle the whole thing by himself, or with only Kelso's help. It would mean moving lots and lots of sand. No, the time was not yet. So he made sure where his wreck was lying and went on to find another wreck site if he could. A lot of people knew where one was, more or less—it lay north of Fort Pierce—but nobody had ever investigated it properly. Now, with his new diving apparatus, he found it, nosed around it, and resurrected a handful of silver coins. Much of the ship was guarded by great heaps of ballast stones. It would be an even greater job to move it all than the first wreck would be. Preparing for that longed-for day when he could actually get to work on it, Wagner applied for and got a salvage (nonexclusive) search lease that covered a region extending from the center of the Sebastian Inlet to a point south of Fort Pierce. He also got exclusive pinpoint leases on the two wrecks he had already investigated, thus proving that though he pictures himself as a greenhorn, he was at least an intelligent greenhorn.

It was 1959–60. By this time, word of Wagner's discoveries had spread among the community, and several men turned up who shared his enthusiasm for treasure hunting. Of the first four, two were expert divers. Very soon they were discussing ways and means, because, as Wagner said, they were all salaried men, raising families, who had no money to throw around. One of them had a friend who worked at Canaveral and owned a twenty-one-foot pleasure boat that seemed right for their purposes. One introduction led to another, until they had an eight-man team, each of whom had some useful skill. Four were expert divers, and soon the others, too, were learning the art. One of the original divers was handy with explosives and electronics, another was trained in law. The boat owner had a good business head. Doc Kelso was their expert in Spanish history and underwater archaeology, and Wagner himself, as he modestly said, had experience in a variety of trades, a strong back, and a tough pair of hands, as well as the enthusiasm to weld the group together.

They were all ready and willing enough, but Wagner knew they needed a lot of training together. After thinking it over, he decided to start them not on one of his two personally discovered wrecks, but on another one that had been well-known for years, just north of Fort Pierce and about twenty miles below Sebastian. It was a decayed skeleton of a galleon about nine hundred feet offshore, in eighteen feet of water.

"I had dived on it myself some years before during my inner-tube days," he said, using the rather odd phrase always employed by divers. He had been an amateur then; the wreck was a kind of proving ground for amateurs, and it was a pretty safe bet that there was nothing there. However, as he said, he wanted to try out his new friends before letting them in on valuable secrets. He had another reason too: If they were really serious they would go on working on this unpromising proposition, but if they were merely out for a lark, the probably barren wreck would test and then discourage them. First, they needed a boat to dive from—not the pleasure boat, though it was fine for general exploration, but a heavier craft, not necessarily fancy or luxurious. One of their number took Wagner to the Navy salvage yards in Norfolk, and for very little money they bought a beat-up forty-foot liberty launch. It was hideous and needed a lot of work, which they did. They christened it the *Sampan* because it looked like a Chinese junk. In April 1960 Kip Wagner decided that they were ready.

The chief part of the wreck's remains was a tremendous heap of ballast rocks, all sizes from quarter pounders to rocks of fifty pounds and more. Clearly they had lined the ship's bottom, beneath the cargo, supplies, and everything else, and even then, after all the years, they described a recognizable outline of the original vessel's bottom. There must have been a hundred tons of rock lying there, Wagner theorized. He had very little hope of finding treasure, but then, that wasn't the real object of the exercise. They dived several times, talked things over, and decided that their only chance of finding anything was to shift the rocks. To begin with, they cut a swathe straight across the midships area; as they had no salvage equipment, the rocks had to be moved by hand. They did this like a bucket brigade, the first man prying loose a rock and passing it between his legs to the one behind him, who passed it on. The third man's job was to pile the rocks in a new place so that they need not be moved again. It was, needless to say, backbreaking work.

By evening they would be completely tired out. Working on the sea bottom used up their air supply much faster than ordinary diving, too, and they had to change the tanks often. When a man was fatigued, he crawled up to the *Sampan*'s deck to catch his breath in the broiling sun. As they cleared the sandy sea bottom they tried pumping the sand off it, and this process called for a better arrangement than they had at first set up. Clearly something else had to be invented to improve the dredge, and they made changes, but it was never very satisfactory. Then too, as the divers all had full-time jobs, the moving of the ballast had to wait for weekends and favorable weather. Still, by midsummer they were bringing up hundreds of shards of Mexican pottery, hundreds of cannonballs, and tiny chips of blue and white porcelain that they only learned later came from rare K'ang-hsi china. Any metallic objects they found were so far gone through oxidization that one couldn't make them out, though they discovered a copper rim and handle and some small brass nails. One thing spurred them on: It was clear that the original Indian divers had not been able to move the ballast. They were the first to try it, so perhaps something in the way of treasure had been left after all.

They needed encouragement, for the summer was running on and some of the men's families were complaining that they never saw them. More than one wife was losing her patience with what she considered romantic schoolboy nonsense. It was Harry Cannon, the owner of the pleasure craft, who broke the jinx one day about the middle of August. He announced that he thought he

saw something, words that left the others cold until he dived
again and found a wedge, like a piece of pie, of some metal that
when scratched showed silver in the light even twenty feet underwater. There it was, a genuine piece of treasure. He looked
around for more until he had six wedges in all; then he came up
to the *Sampan* and handed over his prize.

There was pandemonium. "Everyone whooped and hollered
and stomped around so that I was sure we'd kick a hole in our
boat and sink on the spot," wrote Kip Wagner. It was a happy
day. Forgetting all the rules about stacking the rocks neatly in
new places, they all got to work shoving the ballast around, looking frantically for more treasure. That afternoon they found
three more silver wedges. Fitted together, the nine pieces made
a perfect circle; they had probably been stacked with other pies,
it was agreed, in a long-perished keg, three pies per keg. Each
keg probably weighed about a hundred pounds. During what
remained of the season, the rest of August, they found at least six
more wedges, each, they estimated, worth five to six hundred
dollars. Wagner lost no time getting exclusive rights from the
government to salvage the wreck, but this didn't stop a man who
had worked with him earlier from bringing a friend and trespass-
ing, finding three of the wedges for himself. The trespasser then
offered them to Wagner for sale, and rather than kick up a fuss
and get a lot of unwanted publicity, Kip bought them. One
turned out to be counterfeit.

As was to be expected at that season, the weather now turned
bad and remained bad until January 8, 1961. It was hard on the
team, kicking their heels and waiting for a chance to get back to
their wreck. Wagner had thought they were really finished with
it now; surely no more could be found. But he was wrong. On
January 8 one of the men brought up what is described as two
clusters or clumps overgrown with coral. They proved to be
silver coins stuck together. Then again the weather closed
against the treasure hunters, this time for more than five weeks,
and when at last they returned it was to a landscape transformed
under the water. Sand coated the ocean floor and the cannon.
"Over the years we have, in fact, rarely seen the same ocean floor
configuration twice," commented Wagner.

The divers recommenced their rock hauling and shifting, and

quickly, thanks to a new, more satisfactory sand dredge, they found loose coins. One of the men found a lumpy object that he thought might be another coin cluster, but no scratching revealed the shine of silver or gold, so he decided it was merely a lump of coral and for a while afterward used it underwater for a stool. One day not long afterward there was an emergency; the *Sampan*'s anchor fluke broke. Four men were below, but Wagner in his haste to get out of danger from the reefs almost forgot to call them back. They came up anyway, having heard the boat's engine start. But one of them, to the surprise of the others, insisted on going below one more time, though it was increasingly dangerous, and when he returned he was carrying the purplish lump that his companion had been using to sit on. In the face of scoffing from the others, he insisted that they examine it more closely. Sure enough, it proved to be the biggest cache yet of coins, two thousand of them, worth between thirty and forty thousand dollars. Quite an expensive stool, they all agreed.

Again weather closed in on the eager hunters for a while. During their enforced rest Harry Cannon, the pleasure-boat owner, called a meeting of the eight companions and put a proposition to them. They ought to have a more formal arrangement, he said, now that they were actually beginning to find treasure. A handshake and verbal agreements were all right for less important matters, but "when money comes in the window," said Cannon, "friendship goes out."

Wagner couldn't see it and was somewhat shocked by the thought. But the others agreed with Harry, and after all, what harm could it do? Harry had drawn up a sample corporation charter which he produced. After a lot of talk and explanation, it was signed by all hands. The only thing remaining was to think of a name, and it was Wagner who suggested the Real Eight, the old Spanish name for a piece of eight. (As there were eight of them it seemed eminently suitable.) Kip Wagner was elected president, Dan Thompson executive vice-president and treasurer, and Harry Cannon secretary. Though Wagner in his unworldliness had protested, the arrangement turned out to be a good one, and very necessary. Their president didn't yet realize it, but the Real Eight was going to be big business.

During the many stormy days that followed, the divers could

not control themselves. They had the habit now, and waiting was hard, so they went every day to the beach even when it was no use. They couldn't possibly dive into murky waters and hope to see anything, but it was a good object lesson as to how so much treasure could have lain hidden all those centuries. The sea bottom, which had been three fathoms deep, was now only two fathoms, and the cannon were completely hidden. Obviously the corporation had to invent a new, more efficient dredge against the time when they could get down there again. Besides, they were now working on another site.

For the dredge, they tried one thing after another. By spring 1961 they had a sand pump that worked, but it went so slowly it wasn't practical. They manufactured another contraption, only to learn one morning in May that most of the sand had got itself swept off the site without their help. Hardly had they got started diving, however, when a new storm put most of the load back on. There was nothing for it but to return to the drawing board and, this time, produce a good, reliable dredge. This one really worked, so well that they named it "the hungry beast." Everything—at least everything less than six inches in diameter—was sucked into its maw, to be spewed into a metal basket after passing through a nine-foot-long shaft. (This was at their new site.) In the middle of June they brought up their first coins of the season, thanks to this dredge. They found through experience that the best way to harvest coins was to catch them before they went into the rubber tubing that formed part of the dredge. It wasn't hard, reported Wagner—the coins floated around in a leisurely way, and you had only to cup your hands to catch them. During the summer the divers brought up hundreds of coins, all silver. "Sometimes we worked all day and only recovered 10 or 15 coins; some days we found none; and on other occasions we found hundreds of them," wrote Wagner. "Our workhorse dredge also spit out silver buckles, iron ships' spikes, potsherds and other assorted items. We found, too, about 20 cannon over a 50- to 60-foot area along the reefs."

Now and then when the weather was too bad to work, they returned to the Fort Pierce site where the water was clearer to look again for silver pie wedges. They had no luck there, but in September, when they were just about ready to call it a season, they made one more find, a small cluster of coins. They had now found several thousand pieces of eight and were willing to pause and take stock. It was time, they agreed, to cash in on some of their findings and use the money for some much-needed improvement in conditions. There should be a cabin on the *Sampan,* for one thing, where divers could rest and get warm. They needed new diving suits too. Very carefully, so as not to flood the market, the treasure finders sold a few silver pieces of eight and were delightfully surprised to find how much they were worth: from ten or fifteen to over a hundred dollars apiece. Dated coins in mint condition brought as much as a hundred and fifty, undated ones sold for thirty-five to fifty, and even the worst of them went for ten to fifteen. When they had enough money for their needs, they stopped selling.

Over the winter of 1961, when it was impossible to dive, they simply went swimming offshore, close in when the waves were too rough for boating. One of the men found three or four tops to silver jars that way, and potsherds and blue and white fragments became a commonplace as they ran in and out of the water. But the real find was made by a member who had developed a method of searching a nearby coral reef in shallow water by fanning sand and gravel out of its crevices. One day he went swimming with a toy wooden paddle. He hadn't even brought his scuba gear with him, so he had to duck in and come out very often to breathe. But he kept at it, fanning away, until he saw something bright and round beginning to appear under the sand. At first he thought it was the top of a beer can, but as he worked he realized that it was thicker than that, like a pot lid. At last he nudged it out. It was a battered piece of sculpture, the figure of a moth in silver, evidently the ornamental stopper for a brandy carafe or something of that sort. One thing was certain—it was a *Spanish* stopper.

Inevitably, the *National Geographic* found the treasure finders and signed them up for an exclusive story, but it did not publish immediately. The first installment dealt with the investigation of the Fort Pierce wreck and the discovery of the silver wedges, and in their usual thorough way the magazine did a lot of photography on it. In 1962 one of the photographers came down to Florida to discuss the matter with the Real Eight, and it was decided that the finding of the silver wedges, reenacted, would make a really effective series. Seven or eight of the things were drawn from the Real Eight's bank vault and with a few pieces of eight were put into a wire basket and lowered through the water, where they were carefully scattered on the sandy floor of the ocean. The photos were taken and the props restored to their basket, which was left dangling while the principals went up for lunch. After about an hour, with the weather looking stormy, Harry Cannon suggested that they reclaim the silver and go home. They agreed and began to haul in the basket. It seemed strangely light, and when it broke through the water's surface they could see why: It was empty. What in the world . . . ? Furious yet frightened, some of the divers went down. There was their silver casually scattered on the sand; wave motion had tipped up the basket and spilled it all out. It was recovered, however, and everybody went home.

That season, in 1962, the members did a little scouting for new wrecks to conquer. They tried an underwater sled, but it came to grief by piling up on a heap of rocks. Two of them got themselves towed by the boat so that they could look around at their leisure; the experiment came to a sudden end when they saw a shark looking at them as if tempted by the moving bait. This incident led to the invention of a shark gun, which worked very well except that the shark took off for deeper waters, the gun's spear stuck in his head, and Wagner, who had shot it, had to sacrifice his weapon.

However, plain diving was still very productive. They found two muskets that way, as well as a bronze apothecary jar and a gold-plated jewelry box. One of the divers one day, after sticking his hand inquisitively down the muzzle of a cannon, felt along its underside and found an excrescence of some sort. It was a silver cup and plate firmly cemented to the cannon by coral growth, and it took two of the men three hours of alternate chipping at their prize before they could bring it away. Everyone agreed it was one of the most beautiful of their winnings from the depths of the sea.

The days went by, but there were many stormy ones; indeed, 1962 was an unusually bad year for treasure seekers in the ocean. One should not complain, sighed Kip Wagner, for after all, if that part of the coast had not been unusually stormy and full of razor-sharp coral reefs there would have been no wrecks and no treasure ships, but it *was* a stormy year. He had about decided that there would be no more treasure found until spring. One November day he and his nephew, a nineteen-year-old named Rex Stocker, drove to the beach out of pure habit and started to walk along the sand. Out of habit, too, Wagner carried his metal detector. There had been a good northeaster blow, and one never knew what would turn up. Sure enough, the detector soon gave its signal, and Kip dug up a piece of eight. Fine! The detector led him along, nearer and nearer the water, and he picked up coins at a surprisingly steady pace. In the meantime Rex got bored. He had no metal detector, so he idly climbed the bluff at their backs, near the edge of the high-water mark. Why? Absentmindedly his uncle wondered, and told himself that there were sure as hell no coins up there. Suddenly Rex jumped up and down and began to shout, "Kip! Kip!" He ran as fast as he could down the bluff and over to Wagner, who now saw that something yellow was wrapped around the boy's arm. What was it?

"Look what I found up there in the sand!" yelled Rex into his uncle's ear, handing him a long golden chain. It was genuine gold, there could be no doubt about that, and it was very, very long. Between gasps, Rex explained. It had been lying up there on the bluff in plain sight if you were looking, but he wasn't. The glitter of the sun had flashed into his eyes or he might have stepped straight over it and gone on. What was it doing way up there on the bluff? Kip rubbed his eyes, or, rather, his eyeglasses. The chain was knotted and redoubled. At home when they could apply the family tape measure they found that it measured eleven feet four and a half inches. The links, beautifully wrought, were shaped like flowers; there were 2,176 of them. In all it weighed nearly half a pound. There was a pendant on the thing, a golden dragon (or possibly, thought Wagner, a grasshopper) about two and a half inches long. The back opened, rather like that of a Boy Scout knife, into a small toothpick, and its tail was shaped like a small spoon, perhaps an ear-reamer. What they did not realize at first, because it was clogged with sand, was that the whole creature constituted a whistle. Later expert opinion has just about decided that it belonged to an admiral of the fleet, which Wagner did not guess. We have all seen little boys in sailor suits wearing whistles on cords, haven't we? This golden carved chain, glorious as it was, was merely a grown-up version of that cord and whistle.

No rejoicing, it seems, can be completely untouched by regret, and Stocker's moment of glory was tarnished by a horrid suspicion that he might have passed up another chain. He distinctly remembered that just before he climbed the bluff he felt something twined around one ankle; thinking it was a stalk of waterweed he kicked it off and stepped out of the water. Could it have been another golden chain? Oh, well, it might just as well have been a genuine piece of weed. At any rate, a careful sifting of the sands yielded no more gold.

There remained the delicate question of whose chain it was in actual fact. If finders are keepers, it was Rex's. But the Real Eight wanted above anything to keep it for their collection, so it was agreed that Rex give it up and take instead forty shares in the corporation. Each member contributed five of his shares to make up the forty.

The Real Eight collection was growing beyond the confines of the corporation vaults. It was the intention of the charter members, when they had amassed enough treasure, to set up a museum somewhere not far from the wrecks so that the public could see it all. In the meantime, however—though (as the author says) it sounded ridiculous—they were hard up for working capital. To be sure the intrinsic worth of that gold chain, for one thing, was estimated at anything from thirty to fifty thousand dollars, but it is impossible to make accurate appraisals of such works of art. Anyway, they didn't want to sell it, or any of their other pretty baubles. The situation was alleviated when another partner bought in, and later, in 1964, the Real Eight acquired two more new partners.

In nature things have a way of hitting an average if only one waits long enough. May of 1963 produced very little in the way of encouragement for the treasure hunters, just enough to keep the partners from grumbling too much. They were busy as usual on new equipment inventions. But then, early in June, they struck (or were struck by) a period of unprecedented calm and clarity, when it actually seemed possible to see the limits and boundaries of their prospecting area. "Visibility ranged from 50 to 100 feet," wrote Wagner joyfully.

The actual leased site was 100 by 40 feet, but they had been concentrating on a much smaller plot about twenty feet square, which was so rich in finds that they deliberately went very slowly, moving sand off and examining every inch of it. That day, however, it was all so bright and clear that they resolved to look beyond their particular patch, and it was as well that they did, for they found blocks of coins welded together in such regular shapes that they must have been packed in chests at the time of the wreck. The chests themselves, of course, had rotted away. Evidently these coins were not so tightly packed as some of the earlier clumps discovered because they had been buried in sand the whole time, which protected them from chemical and physical action. A lot of them slipped out of the clumps as they were being carried up to the top of the water, and when the divers went down again to "vacuum" the sea bed they discovered a handsome silver crucifix as well. Fortunately, the weather stayed calm for several days, allowing the adventurers to uncover a new kind of treasure, a cache of K'ang-hsi china cups and bowls, still as carefully packed as when they were stowed on board. There were twenty-eight in all of these perfect specimens, and, of course, many more in the form of fragments. These too were accompanied by pieces of Mexican pottery. Later, when the Real Eight wrote to an authority on pottery, Mrs. Kammar Aga Oglu at the University of Michigan, and described their find, she told them that the china they had found was exported in vast numbers at the time of the Plate Fleet to be sold cheap, like five-and-dime china today. Its value now, of course, is vastly increased. The Victoria and Albert Museum in London has declared it priceless. On another day they found a second gold chain hidden in a cannon's mouth where it could not possibly have started the voyage. Attached to it was a miniature painting, but the colors and design under the glass cover had long since washed away.

The success story was still exciting, but there were two drawbacks. For one thing—though they may not have felt this way; it is probably more my reaction than Kip Wagner's—what they had found so far, save for the chains, was silver, not gold. For another, at the rate they were going they would never finish their explorations. It was all very well to be thorough, but if they had to leave a large part of their claim unexamined, it was frustrating. Again, the Real Eight never quite voiced their misgivings on this point, but a third party came along at the right time and put it into words. The two points hang together, so let us begin with the entry of Mel Fisher into the story.

Fisher was a professional treasure hunter and diver who went anywhere that promised rewards for his peculiar talents. He had dived, for example, into some of the famous *cenotes* (ancient water tanks) of Yucatán after the Mayan treasure rumored to be lying there. Possibly, however, he made more money out of a shop he opened in California, where divers could buy the latest thing in gear rather than treasure. On a trip to a diving spot near Puerto Rico, he stopped by to meet the Real Eight. Kip Wagner made him welcome and showed him some maps. Fisher thought things over and came up with a proposition: Why shouldn't he hire a team of professional divers to help the Florida men? They would dive on the Real Eight's leased sites every day instead of only weekends, which were the Real Eight's only diving days, and in return for permission to do this, they would split the value of anything they found halfway down the middle after the state had taken its 25 percent. If the board agreed, he would get busy and sign up the divers, who would be asked to work the first year without pay, gambling on finding something to make it worth their while. So it was agreed.

The diving season of 1963 was well under way when they got the news that Mel Fisher was coming, complete with his gang of divers. The advance messenger, Rupert Gates, went out with some members of the Real Eight on a trial run aboard the *Sampan;* it was a nice sunny day for diving. Almost immediately they found a few pieces of eight and, later, some silver forks. The men had stopped to rest when two of them decided to try out one more spot. And then at last it happened: One of them found "a beautiful eight-escudo piece as perfect and fresh as the day it had been minted." Needless to say, it was a gold coin. In fact, it was the first gold coin that anyone in the Real Eight had as yet turned up. The two men who found it said they were working in eight feet of water when all of a sudden the sand slid away, parting like the Red Sea, and it was as if someone had turned a flashlight in their eyes. The floor was covered with gold coins. Now they all got busy, forming a circle around the area and working in. (Gates was with them; it was an extraordinary introduction for him to the Florida diving field.) In all, they found twenty-three coins before the weather got too rough for diving—doubloons, four- and eight-escudo pieces, all together. One of the men also got a heavy gold ring which he saw slipping down a sandy slope; he simply stuck his finger under it and let it slide on. Certainly it all lent a fillip to the proceedings. There is nothing like gold to whet the appetite.

"I once found a gold coin," said the lady in charge today of the Real Eight Museum at Canaveral. "I was out with a bunch of people, coin hunting more or less on the beach—we do a lot of that around here—and because it was high tide we were making our way around the high-water mark on the bluff. I was holding on with one hand, because the path was narrow and the bluff was steep, when all of a sudden I saw this coin in the water, turning over and over at the top of the wave the way things do. Well, I leaned out and grabbed a handful of the water and whatever was in it, and then I was too busy to look at what I had. I wasn't sure I'd caught it until we got past that place and were on level land. Then I opened my hand, and there it was."

In August 1963, operations were varied by the appearance of three men who had gold coins that were obviously from the Fleet; they claimed to have found them in the water, which was important. If they had been found on the beach it made a differ- ence; they could have come from anywhere. In the water, of course, their presence pointed to a wreck site. Wagner asked various questions and the answers indicated that the wreck site, if they had indeed found one, was not included in his list. They wanted to come to an agreement with the Real Eight, taking a percentage of whatever might be found thanks to their discov- ery. In the course of time these men were a great nuisance. They finally admitted, when cornered, that the coins had indeed come from the beach; they had learned Wagner's name and address from a coin dealer in New York who recognized the gold coins' provenance from their mint marks. But by that time they felt they had a claim on whatever was found, and they brought suit against the Real Eight. They lost their case, but it all took time.

Mel Fisher's team found only just enough to keep them hanging on in 1963, but 1964 brought its reward. One of Fisher's team had a gadget that had taken him two years to invent and perfect; it was called a *magnetometer* and was more than useful for finding metal in water. Another tool, designed by Fisher himself, was called a *blaster,* for the reason that when turned onto a piece of ground it sent everything flying in a cloud of sand, creating a kind of waterfall down which the detritus slipped. In April, with the blaster and the magnetometer, Real Eight's divers along with Fisher's team, working a new site, turned up about a hundred pieces of eight. Then on May 8 one of Fisher's men, working alone, found two golden discs weighing seven pounds apiece. On May 21 they got more than two hundred gold coins.

On May 24 what Kip Wagner called the big haul was made. Mel's blaster had cut a hole about 15 feet by 5 or 6 feet. A diver named Moe with two other divers went down to see it and were blinded—really blinded—by a bright yellow glow. There, said Wagner, "was a veritable carpet of gold." Moe grabbed two fistfuls and surfaced.

It was easier said than done. Even underwater gold is very heavy, and the golden coins were slippery; they were apt to fall out of a diver's grip. When this happened it was not easy to find them again because they were immediately covered with a thin layer of sand. The blaster was left going to keep the treasure exposed, but it also fought against the divers, who had to go on kicking and thrashing about just to stay where they were, picking gold like buttercups in a meadow. The old bucket-squad technique was too dangerous on that busy plot of sand. A diver simply picked up a handful of coins, stuffed them into the cuff of a glove he wore on his other hand, grabbed as many more as he could carry, and went upstairs to unload. They got sixty to eighty pieces each time like that. Afraid the weather might change, nobody paused for coffee or food; they hardly stopped to rest, though it was grueling work. By the end of the day the men's wrists, where they had stuffed the gold pieces, were bleeding, but they had collected 1,033 gold coins. It was a record-breaking day. Next day they found nine hundred gold doubloons. In a week they recovered about twenty-five hundred. Then, as all things must, it came to an end. Evidently the gold had all been found, though a few scattered coins did turn up from time to time. Elsewhere they found a small gold pendant portraying a saint's head.

On another day, at Fort Pierce, they found a silver bar weighing more than thirty-five pounds. Other gold discs were recovered, along with a silver one. It was agreed that these were a form of ingot; some had mint and assayer's marks on them.

Hurricanes closed the diving season late in August, but the men were not inclined to grumble. Counting up their winnings for 1964 was a pleasant occupation: more than thirty-seven hundred gold coins, over two hundred pounds of pieces of eight, six silver and six gold discs, the silver bar, sixteen gold rings, eight pieces of golden chain, several pieces of silver cutlery (knives, forks, and spoons), two silver candlestick tops, and two silver plates. There were also a number of interesting artifacts—cannon, cannonballs, sounding leads, pewter plates, musket balls, and various jars, even a sword handle and part of its blade.

One problem that faced them was the discoloration of the silver pieces of eight. Nobody looking at these black or brownish fragments corroded with silver sulfide would think much of them; they had to be cleaned up. The treasure hunters and their wives tried scrubbing them with everything they could think of, steel wool, acid, sand, soda—nothing was satisfactory. It was true that a person could eventually turn out a shining silver coin, but at the cost of the skin on his hands. Finally they rigged up a box that was rotated by electric power, put in some silver coins along with a handful of steel shot and some detergent, and turned it on. Round and round went the box, rattling loudly. At last! After a certain amount of this buffeting, the silver came out bright.

After making their inventory, the divers talked things over. In spite of all that treasure in the vaults, they were hard up. Though they knew it would be unwise to unload too much gold and silver on the market, they decided to risk just a bit as a trial balloon, and some of their prize pieces, accordingly, were sent to a coin auction being held in October in New Jersey. One gold coin, a "beautiful eight-escudo piece," the best of the collection, was put up for sale first. They had estimated it at four thousand dollars; it went for thirty-five hundred. Not a bad guess, Wagner said to himself, and he took heart. Another coin outdid it, going to a

Spanish dealer for thirty-six hundred—and the buyer was later quoted as calling it a steal.

In all they sold a hundred coins, from which they realized $29,000. When all outstanding debts had been settled and each man's expenses paid, the rest of the money was divided according to agreement. Some had a few thousand to show for it, one or two only a thousand dollars. It seemed ironic, as Wagner commented, that though they had recovered treasure probably worth millions, they were able to pocket only a few thousand dollars. But presumably it was a temporary state of affairs, one of the small trials of dealing in a managed market where one's commodity had a scarcity value.

In the end the treasure finders did not lose out, but they were to go through a lot of trials first. Outstanding among these were the activities of a new and voracious collector for Florida's Internal Improvement Fund, a man aptly named Kidd. Real Eight had carefully complied with the laws regarding leases and claims, not so much out of innate virtue as from caution, but Kidd could not believe that they were within the law, what with all that gold being brought up from Florida waters. He was determined to find corruption somewhere, somehow, so as to profit from it. Jumping the gun, after the manner of politicians, he jubilantly announced to the public that through the efforts of his department the state had probably been saved two or three hundred thousand dollars which would otherwise have gone into the coffers of Real Eight and the Treasure Salvors, as Mel Fisher's outfit was called, and that this was just the beginning. At this point the business-wise Harry Cannon stepped in and threatened to sue the state for a genuine fortune, the sum of $25 million being bandied about just to start with; the officials now came down to earth and stopped issuing statements like Kidd's. The smoke cleared away and a new contract was signed to clear up the matter. From then on, new treasure hunters could come into the tract formerly leased by Wagner, but the divers of Real Eight had a renewable six-year contract for their particular eight wreck sites, and this, with options, was to run to 1975. No change was made in the arrangement by which the state of Florida received 25 percent of the value of anything salvaged. In earlier days the kings of Spain claimed only a fifth of the gold mined within her American empire, and as we have seen they seldom actually got it. Florida had a better deal all round.

Now at last the *National Geographic* took the wraps off the story and began sending out advance publicity. Wagner and his friends were not exactly delighted. Naturally the brouhaha brought fortune hunters in from miles around. People carrying brand-new metal detectors crowded the beaches; Wagner said that one morning after a storm he counted fourteen such seekers hard at work. "Most of them wouldn't have recognized a piece of eight if it had dropped into their hands," he said with genial scorn. The beaches were public property, but their wreck sites were not, and all day long the divers had to shoo intruders out of the shallower waters that covered their claims. There were even boats drifting quite openly over the marked sites.

Shops and mail-order houses dealing in diving gear and metal detectors were constantly having to reorder stock. People paid through the nose for diving lessons so that they could use their beautiful new diving suits. A book by John Potter, *The Treasure Diver's Guide,* sold out in no time, and local public libraries had to take the volume out of circulation. (A less helpful book, the *World Treasure Atlas,* was nearly sold out when I visited the Real Eight Museum in 1979. I got the last copy, but I must admit I would be hard put to make my fortune out of it.) Then there was the map of sunken treasure ships; thousands of copies of this chart have been sold, with no discoverable results except the enrichment of the printer.

There were more legal hassles as the years went by, but they did not interfere with the treasure seekers' main activity, diving. One result of the disputes between the Real Eight with their associates and the state was a so-called Antiquities Commission, which covers treasure troves, marine salvage, artifacts, historic sites and objects, fossil deposits, documents, books, and all other personal or real property of scientific and historic value. The commission was set up as well to help arrange for the salvage, protection, and preservation of all the sites and objects covered by the law. The state continues to take a 25 percent bite of all findings, but various new regulations have made it more difficult for just anybody to wander in and start treasure hunting. Leases

are required, and they are not easy to get: Applicants must show
some reason for thinking that they will find treasure. Naturally,
the commission had to set up a patrol to make sure the new laws
were followed. In the meantime, Real Eight and Fisher went on
with their explorations.

In 1964 the *Sampan,* never an ideal divers' craft, was declared
practically unseaworthy, and the men found a replacement in an
uglier and even more awkward—but serviceable—scowlike vessel they named the *Derelict.* They worked on it whenever diving
was impracticable, and in the process they invented an improvement on Mel Fisher's blaster, a powerful machine that could not
only blast away sand and mud with terrific strength, but throttle
down to a comparatively gentle current that uncovered prizes
without hurting them or blowing them away. It was far more
effective than they could have hoped; Wagner said it cut years
off their salvage operations, but they were not to know that, of
course, until they tried it out. All they knew, when at last it was
ready in April 1965, was that they had worked harder than would
seem possible ever since July 1964, and that they had sunk fifteen
thousand dollars in it.

April marked the beginning of the new diving season. They
went out full strength, augmented by three youngsters, Rex (who
had found the eleven-foot gold chain) and two companions.
There was plenty of work for all, they agreed; both the cabin site,
as they called their second working place, and the one at Fort
Pierce kept yielding steady supplies of gold and silver in the
shape of coins. Finally Bob Johnson, one of the divers, quit his
weekday job to be master of the *Derelict;* to finance this venture,
Real Eight sold more of their coins and borrowed from the bank,
putting up doubloons as collateral. The *Derelict* was put to work
on April 22. The first finds made off her deck were merely two
silver coins and part of a silver candlestick, but everyone took this
rather skimpy prize as a good omen, and Bob Johnson nailed one
of the cobs (a cob is a silver coin) to the cabin wall as a hopeful
sign of better things to come.

Day after day, for nearly a month, the *Derelict* sailed out with
her three young divers and her master, to anchor near known
wrecks wherever the weather seemed propitious. It meant a
good deal of wandering around; a mild spot might give way to a

stormy one in the space of a few minutes. On May 19 they were near the Fort Pierce wreck, after a day in which nothing had been found. It was almost time, thought Johnson, to call a halt, especially when their least experienced diver, Bob Conkey, complained that it was inky black underwater and he couldn't see anything. The other two agreed. But even as they talked, Johnson as ship's master thought he saw a break here and there in the blackness, and he got ready to dive once more, just to be sure. "Keep on trying," he told the youngsters. "Find clear spots and work them there if you can."

Obediently they dived again. It was Conkey who came up waving a gold doubloon triumphantly in his fist, and everybody went at his work again with new enthusiasm. That day they found nineteen gold coins, and during the next few days they salvaged more, with pewter plates, cannon, and two anchors.

One could never be sure, emphasized Wagner, that he had encompassed the whole area of a wreck. The violence of that fatal storm and the rough wave action that followed sometimes spread a ship's remains far and wide. The site where the young divers found all those doubloons was a long way from Mel Fisher and his Salvors, but they were all working profitably on the same ship nevertheless. It was, too, a matter of luck, said Kip. Some people have it and some don't. One of his divers, Del Long, had luck. Whenever he had a hunch the others, if they knew what was good for them, followed it. He had just such a hunch one Sunday when all of them were together.

"I've got a feeling," he said, "that we're going to hit it big again soon—right over there," and he indicated a place about nine hundred feet south of the spot where they were diving. Johnson and two of the others followed his directions and dived—and found 130 golden coins four fathoms down. This was enough for them to agree that they should all dive next day even though it was Monday, not a usual day for activity en masse.

"We sailed at 8:48 A.M., and anchored a little over an hour later, about 1,000 feet offshore," wrote Wagner. "Within 20 minutes Conkey came up with a gold doubloon. He had opened the floodgates to the most fantastic single day we have ever recorded." Wagner had lately suffered from a bad back and was taking it easy, but that day he could not resist joining the others.

Visibility was good, forty or fifty feet in all directions. Conditions were perfect. The sands were dazzlingly white.

Their blaster had cut a big hole about thirty feet in diameter, and through it they saw many pieces of gold. Some of the coins lay in neat stacks of three and four. Water magnified them, so it looked as if the sea bottom was veritably lined with gold. The divers were all motionless for a space, overawed by the sight. When at last they moved, it was not to grab at the gold immediately; they went up to the *Derelict* and called down their friends, making sure everyone could see it before it was spoiled.

There were so many coins that they scooped them up by handfuls and loaded buckets to the brim with them. They were in mint condition, most of them the big eight-escudo size. All day long the divers poured a steady torrent of gold onto the deck of the *Derelict.*

When they quit they believed that they had found more treasure in one day than anyone else in history. The total count, when they had made it, finger-sore and with dazzled eyes, was 1,128 coins including 518 eight-escudo pieces, which in those days were valued at from a thousand to three thousand dollars apiece.

The weather made it impossible to go out the next few days: June 3 was the earliest they could dare the elements, and then they found only a few more gold coins—six, and five on June 4. So it went until they concluded that they had cleaned out the wreck of that particular hoard, which, they agreed, had almost certainly been contained in one chest, all together. Theorizing further, they decided that the place they had made the incredible find probably represented a portion of the ship that had broken away and been flung into the crevice between the first and second coral reefs. Cannon had been found nearby, but there was no ballast. No, the rest of the wreck was the site where they had found their first gold coins, the K'ang-hsi china, and the pieces of eight, among the ballast rocks. The divers worked out a chart of where the main part of the wreck might well be and then set to work to locate it with the magnetometer. A few days later, working by the chart, they anchored the *Derelict* over the deeper spot where, with luck, the wreck site might be. Triumph! Within nine minutes the divers on their first trip brought up silver wedges like those found in 1960; there were three of these.

Nine more were found that day, as well as three clumps of silver coins, several hundred other pieces of eight, and *ten* silver discs of varying thickness, weighing from 44 to 105 pounds apiece. It was very hard to haul these up, but nobody complained.

In addition they salvaged a mystery object, a round-bottomed bottle, still sealed and carrying some sort of liquid. But it was the amount of silver they now found that made the location remarkable. They had recovered less in all of 1960 and 1961 than they now carried out of the seabed in one day. The tally on the following day was several thousand loose silver coins. On June 14 there were so many that they were simply weighed instead of counted —665 pounds of coinage. There were also twelve more silver wedges, eight more of the heavy metal discs, two silver "biscuit-shaped chunks," and a clump of coins.

From then on, as Wagner said, it got damn near ridiculous. In about a week they had brought up nearly a ton of pieces of eight alone. There were so many that Bob Johnson told the boys to skip picking up loose coins and concentrate on finding bars, discs, wedges, and other large items. It was a long time since Kip Wagner had found his first black piece of eight on the beach and was happy to have done so.

The Real Eight decided to apply scientific principles to their new site, at least as scientific as possible. They used a grid system and mapped out the territory, marking each square once it had been carefully investigated. More and more finds were made. They called in Mel Fisher and his Treasure Salvors to help bring up the silver, and all of them moved, slowly, patiently, and perhaps inexorably, across the chart. They even began to feel bored as the torrent of silver kept clanking down on deck. (The ship, they felt sure, was the *capitana* of the Silver Fleet.) One day Rex Stocker came up unusually quickly: "Mr. Johnson, there's a chest of silver down there," he reported. Practical joking was the crew's favorite pastime, and Johnson refused to be drawn. "If you say so," he replied. "Go on down and bring it up."

Nobody had ever seen a wooden chest in the wreck sites. Wood from the fleet was unknown, the teredo worms having long since eaten every scrap. But Rex insisted that he was telling the truth: There really was a chest down there, full of silver. He was persuasive enough, at last, to get Del Long to come down with him for a look, and Long came up almost immediately, saying that it was true; there was a chest down there, just as Rex had said. After that, of course, everybody went to have a look—"a blackish-colored wooden container," Wagner described it, "about three feet long, a foot or so wide, and about a foot deep." One end and the lid were missing; otherwise the chest seemed intact, which was amazing. And it was, indeed, full of silver. The divers went into a huddle and agreed that every effort must be made to bring the chest up undamaged. It probably weighed in the neighbor-hood of two hundred pounds and would of course need careful handling. First the chest had to be worked loose, ever so gently, of the sand that had covered it and preserved it from the teredos. This undertaking took four hours. When it was completed, a piece of plywood was slid carefully underneath and the whole arrangement was lifted with lines, a man watching every corner in order to protect it. As soon as the chest was safely landed on deck it was immersed in a tub of water. Otherwise, Wagner explained, the sun would dry it out of shape and even rot it. It was lined with lead. The pieces of eight were clotted in clumps, fused together like so many others, but the number was es-timated at about one thousand.

The 1965 diving season soon came to an end with a hurricane, but the divers were satisfied with their year, and with good rea-son.

It was early spring 1979 when I visited the beach near Canav-eral. Though there were few picnic parties around, I knew—because I had tried to book nearer to the museum—that practi-cally all the ocean-front motels were occupied. There is no season in Florida any more in the old-fashioned sense of the word. Peo-ple just live there as Kip Wagner and his friends did, or at least visit it whenever the notion strikes them. The room I found was eight miles away by taxi meter.

The Museum of Sunken Treasure, 8625 Astronaut Boulevard, is located in its own building, a round, handsome structure over-looking (of course) the sandspit that is the beach, across Astronaut Boulevard, and the sea beyond it.

The museum probably started with an exhibit put on by the *National Geographic* in their Explorers' Hall in Washington, which featured all the special treasures already disinterred—the eleven-foot chain and whistle, the K'ang-hsi china, some gold discs and silver wedges, and so forth. Record-breaking crowds surged in; sometimes the line of people waiting outside was two blocks long. Some were repeaters, coming back again and again to stare. The exhibit moved on after that to the Florida State Museum in Gainesville, with the same staggering response from the public. In autumn 1964, the Real Eight, at a board meeting, decided that this exhibit ought to have a permanent home of its own, and plans were quickly made to set it up at Harry Cannon's bank at Satellite Beach, thirty-five miles north of Sebastian. Later they built their own building not far away—but perhaps this was not a good idea, as things turned out.

At first the show was mouth-watering. By the time I got there, however, change had overtaken it. "We had a robbery, you know. *Two* robberies, as a matter of fact," said the curator as I stared at an empty exhibition case. "No, they didn't get the golden chain with the whistle; fortunately that had already been sold. But as you see, they took the imitation one, and the K'ang-hsi porcelain, and some coins. We have a better alarm system now—at least I hope so. You'd have thought nobody could have gotten in, the way it was, but they did. Well, such as it is, there's the exhibition."

The case from which the imitation admiral's whistle chain was taken now sports a color photograph of the artifact. There are coins in the shop, some genuine, some clever imitation. There are bags of small ballast stones, certified genuine; I bought one. The unopened "onion" flask is still there, and so are some chips of china and pottery, but it is inside the museum, at the general exhibition, that the visitor gets a truer picture of the overall set-up—wrecks, rocks, and all. Through a circular hallway he is led past solid, not very convincing seascapes, full of plaster coral reefs and rocking ships, to a realistic underwater scene, properly lit, where you can stare your fill at the sandy bottom with here and there a gold coin. On the other end is the Mint Room, showing minting techniques of the eighteenth century, the Storm Room, the Treasure Room, and, still carefully encased in clean fresh water, the chest, full of silver coins or reasonable simulacra. (If I were running that museum I would leave nothing of value in it.) In another chest is an attractive lot of various coins as they were brought up from the deep (or, more likely, imitation coins).

"I'm afraid the museum is a sad joke nowadays," said a Florida resident later. "It's a pity, but then the Real Eight came to an end in 1975 and disbanded, and there's nobody to keep an eye on things any more. Kip Wagner died of cancer. The K'ang-hsi china? Well, if you ask me, it's probably lying in a safe belonging to one of the directors right now."

Nobody, I reflected, shrinks from calling a spade a spade in Florida, but never mind. I resolved to go back and look at the museum all over again next day. Phony or not, there was something about all that glitter. . . .

10

GOLDEN WATER

Most Americans are familiar, however vaguely, with the story of the forty-niners and the nineteenth-century gold rushes of North America, but they may not be aware that it wasn't a simple discovery that started it all at Sutter's Mill, as the schoolbooks have it. Americans who lived in the California territory knew long before 1849 that the land was auriferous in places, but if they also knew what was good for them or the nation, they kept quiet about it. The awkward fact was that California was not at that time a part of the United States but belonged to Mexico. We were at war with Mexico from 1846 to 1848 over our annexation of Texas, which ended with California's being annexed as well, but until then the territory and the gold in it were Mexican, and nobody could dispute it. So Americans were fairly quiet about such matters.

Not everybody else maintained the same cautious attitude. In 1816 an English mineralogist published a book in which he referred perfectly candidly to the gold in California's mountains; did this hint at ideas in British heads about some day occupying that lovely territory? Some Americans thought it did, and they stared resentfully across the Atlantic toward England. The French, too, were suspected of entertaining unlawful designs on California.

No, the gold was no secret. It was well known, for instance, though not said aloud very often, that a trapper, prospecting in the Sierra Nevadas in 1826, panned for gold and found plenty of it. Indians traded with gold dust in Pacific ports. Ships that stopped at these ports on their way east around the Horn would

take on gold, which the officers sold without fanfare along the
Atlantic seaboard. But nobody made a fuss about it until, in 1843
and again in 1844, the tiresome yellow stuff turned up in more
than paying quantities on John Sutter's ranch at Coloma in California, and he had a lot of trouble hushing it up. Not that he had
any objection to gold as gold, but the Mexican War was approach-
ing, he was not sure of his position as a settler, and he wanted to
make a success of his homestead. He was obviously a provident
fellow, not inclined to go haring off after fortunes.

James Marshall, who had been hired by Sutter to build a sawmill on his land, was a different type; some might say he was more
normal, because when he found gold, as he did almost immediately on January 24, 1848, he was excited. He told his employer,
and Sutter said yes, he knew there was gold there, but he had his
reasons for keeping quiet, and he explained them. He said Marshall would oblige him by shutting up, at least until the status of
California was settled. Negotiations were under way for ending
the hostilities; the United States had won the war and, in fact, the
treaty was signed only nine days later, on February 2. Sutter
asked Marshall to carry on with building the mill as he had been
hired to do. He and his crew could look for gold, if that was what
they wanted, after hours in their own time, but not during the
working day. Sutter said that when the mill was finished they
could do what they liked about announcing their find; he would
even grubstake them if they carried out their part of the bargain.
But the mill had to be finished first.

It was a reasonable request, but when it comes to gold people
are not reasonable. Look, for example, at the way one of Sutter's
good friends behaved. The friend happened to be starting out for
Monterey, and Sutter asked him, while he was there, to investigate the Sutter title to his land. Incautiously he also mentioned
that gold had been found there, but after all, this was a *friend*.
Nevertheless, the word *gold* pushed the thought of Sutter's title
out of the friend's mind; even their friendship seems to have
gone by the board. In Monterey the man made friends with an
experienced prospector and learned from this veteran something of mining techniques. As soon as he got back home he built
for himself a cradle, or rocker. This is a tool one step up in
complexity from the primitive pan immortalized in Western

movies as part of the gold hunter's outfit, along with his mule. The pan, as almost nobody needs telling, is exactly that, a kind of pie-baking dish about three or four inches deep. Using it was a slow and somewhat slapdash method and probably served better as an indication of gold than as a serious gold extractor. The cradle was an improvement, being a box of wood three feet long or so, on rockers. It was made deliberately higher at one end than the other, and across the bottom of the interior were thin strips of wood or perhaps wool—shades of the Golden Fleece—to catch the gold dust. The water-sand-dust mixture was poured into the cradle at the high end, the box was rocked, the stuff was separated by gravity, and the water and silt came out at the other end, leaving the gold, if any, caught on the wood or woolen strips called riffles. But an ordinary cradle, too, sometimes lacked efficiency, proving too short to make the desired separation in the time it afforded one particle to travel from head to foot. So the miners built a longer box, as much as ten feet long, and if they could run a steady stream of water through it, sluicing it, they need not bother to construct rockers at all. This elongated, rockerless cradle was known as a *long tom,* and it simplified the miners' work. In due course they found it even more effective, given a good source of sluicing water, to build a series of long toms, but often the necessary water was lacking for such an operation.

Sutter's erstwhile friend settled down with his rocker on Sutter's land to carry out his research, and the building crew, seeing what he was doing, quickly made cradles for themselves, one by one. They stopped even pretending to work on the sawmill, and it never did get finished. Other gold seekers joined them without asking Sutter's leave, camping there until his ranch was swamped with strangers who used his livestock and, all day long, panned or cradled for gold. Usually they found it, too, but stubborn Sutter was ruined.

The word spread quickly. Soon Monterey and Yerba Buena, later to be christened anew as San Francisco, were deserted. Shops were closed, houses left empty, doors swung in the wind —everybody was off to Coloma after gold. The craze spread and the world moved in on the hills of California; settlers from Oregon joined the rush, as did Hawaiians, Mexicans, South Ameri-

cans, and Australians. Oddly enough, communications being so
bad, people in eastern North America were rather late hearing
of the gold strike. Official word did not come to them until De-
cember 5, nearly a year after the rush started, when President
Polk, who had received a tin can full of nuggets and a letter from
officials in the West, informed Congress of the discoveries that
had devastated Sutter's Mill. Immediately the population of the
East rose up in thousands and started out to California to join the
other gold grubbers.

Not all northeastern Americans went, of course—not quite all.
It was a long way off and the trip was fraught with difficulties.
Those who were not foolhardy waited until the beginning of
spring in the new year. Forty thousand Americans journeyed
overland to California, mostly by wagon; thirty-five thousand
went by ship, some rounding the Horn but more disembarking
at Panama, where they crossed the Isthmus—a journey harder
than it sounds—and embarked again on any craft they could find
that was sailing north. Any method, by land or sea, was rugged,
and what the hopeful travelers found when they arrived at Yerba
Buena or some other coast settlement was a state of affairs like
nothing they had ever before known. In the interim between
winning the war and setting up a government for California,
nobody was in charge; there was no governing body and no book
of laws. The prospectors were in a hurry and didn't bother about
such things except insofar as their own homemade laws applied
to claims on gold-bearing land. There, of course, men and women
were jealous of their rights and watched their rivals like hawks.

In a way it wasn't bad. The advantage of living in a legislative
vacuum was chiefly that whatever gold you had was yours and
only yours—as long as you could hang on to it. In those halcyon
times you didn't have to buy a license or a lease. Better, there was
no king, no court to claim a royal fifth. All you had to do was walk
out and pick the stuff up—if it was there, of course, and at first
there was quite a lot of it for the taking. As the easy gold was used
up, people looked farther and farther afield, and as they moved
on, others watched them, promptly picked up their traps, and
followed. For some time California was populated by the largest
group of nomads seen in the world since the days of the Thracians
and their relatives who wandered over Asia.

Those were the palmy days, when nature and erosion did the hard work. Inevitably, however, placer mining comes to an end and the miner must look for the original vein or veins from which the gold came. It began to be more difficult to get it even when the vein, or lode, was found; the rock had to be broken up and the question arose how to pick up the gold even then. They roasted the debris to melt gold; they tried chlorination, which worked—at a price—but takings fell off until some chemists in Scotland invented the cyanide method in 1887. Both potassium and sodium cyanide like gold, or, in scientific language they have an affinity for it, and vice versa. Solutions of these cyanides, run through crushed gold ore, came out with the gold attached, and were then treated with zinc. This caused the fickle cyanides to drop their gold burden in order to unite with the zinc, and there you were with a fine-grained, slimy black substance that was gold in spite of its unappetizing appearance. It was a cheap method and soon paid off. In Australia the miners watched the success of cyanidization in America and were soon imitating it, with good results all round.

Gina Allen in her book *Gold!* describes what happened to the army of amateur miners as they wandered about looking for prizes:

They spread themselves through the Sierra Nevadas along what the Mexican miners called the Veta Madre, or Mother Lode. On the edges of cliffs, in gullies and inaccessible canyons, they staked their claims and built their tent-and-shack communities. Some of these sprang up one week and were ghost towns the next, as news of a richer strike lured away the fortune hunters. Nothing could be kept secret along the Mother Lode. It was said that a story told in Mariposa, at the southern end of the gold territory, would be repeated in Downieville, two hundred miles to the north, within two hours. The human grapevine took the place of telephone, telegraph, and newspaper.

Over it spread the report of the nugget found near Carson Hill. It weighed 195 pounds and was valued at $74,000. North of Carson Hill, at Angel's Camp, a prospector named Raspberry, who had found no gold, went out to hunt for meat. He had trouble with his gun, struck it against a rock, which broke away revealing signs of gold. By himself he dug $7,000 worth of ore in three days, opening the mine which eventually made him a millionaire.

In Grass Valley, George Knight found a fortune by stubbing his toe on a piece of gold-bearing quartz that proved to be an outcrop of a rich underground vein. At another mining camp the prospectors stopped work to bury one of their number. As they bowed their heads while the volunteer preacher prayed, they saw the sheen of gold in the open grave. The service stopped abruptly, the coffin was removed and the mourners staked claims and began digging.

There were some prospectors, Ms. Allen sums up, who made fortunes in the California rush, often as the result of chance accidents. Other men found enough to win them fifty to five hundred dollars a day. When they had worked out their claims, the sensible ones who had saved their money were able to retire and live comfortably, but a larger number didn't find any of these goodies and were lucky if they made expenses. On the average, a man found about an ounce of gold a day. This, sold at an assay office and depending on its purity, was worth from twelve to sixteen dollars. If it was traded rather than sold, it was worth only about half that much; with eggs costing a dollar apiece, if they were available at all, an omelette for a man with a hearty appetite would use up all his day's wages. That was why flapjacks were popular: They were made without eggs, of sourdough. A pinch of gold dust, says Gina Allen, was worth about a dollar, and clerks and bartenders with large thumbs were in demand by employers, as their pinch was bigger.

The original lawless state did not persist; instead, the miners themselves formed a kind of democracy, which varied with the locality. Reports Ms. Allen:

As a strike was made, and prospectors gathered in number, they met together and agreed on laws for the new district, the boundaries of which varied with its fortunes. These laws regulated the size and number of claims each man could locate, the way they should be marked and protected from trespassers, the actions that were to be considered crimes and their punishment. Town meetings were held on Sunday, when most of the prospectors were in camp. The majority ruled and the decision was final. Since there were no jails, crimes were punished immediately. Theft was the most heinous offense. A man accused of stealing tools or provisions from another's claim could be tried, convicted, and hanged within an hour. If the crime was a lesser one, the culprit might be banished from the district. Sometimes he was branded, that his criminal record should be known to those he met later.

The author adds that the laws made by the miners of 'forty-nine pertaining to mining and mineral rights form the basis of the rules governing the mining industry throughout the United States today. This much they could boast if they were still alive, but they cannot boast of having invented new mining methods. Panning, cradling, and even "hydraulicking," as it was called in the West, were as we know an old story when the Romans dug their gold. The forty-niners, too, used water force, washing away mountains of dirt just as it was done in Spain, with equally horrifying results. Today there is a law against it in California, now that it is too late.

By 1859, men had taken $555 million worth of gold from Californian ground, $135 million more than the Spaniards got out of the Americas in a century.

From then on, discoveries of gold proliferated, as was inevitable. The world shrinks, discoveries increase, techniques improve, and knowledge is stored up. After the first North American gold strikes—which went on and on through the next few decades, including the Klondike adventure—came Australia.

The beginning of gold mining in that subcontinent makes a good story. One of the Australians who came rushing to California among the other forty-niners was a man named E. H. Hargraves, who was not a convict like so many others in his country, but an Englishman who had come out as a youth to seek adventure in Australia and make his fortune. He went to California in the same spirit and had no more luck than he had had on his first attempt in the Antipodes, but he did gain something more valuable—experience. He recognized the looks of the country; he might as well have been in his own back yard. If Australia didn't have gold, he told himself, he was very much mistaken. Without wasting too much time in America he returned, in 1851, to the Macquarie River district in New South Wales and began looking for gold in all the likely places along the river and its tributaries that he could spot. And, wonder of wonders, he found gold—lots of it.

The Australian officials were rather slow to respond. In that country of convicts, they told each other, the lawlessness inherent in gold discovery might well wreak havoc. But as some of them argued, a lot of their good solid citizens too were slipping away, lured by the gold of America; wouldn't it be as well to claim what was theirs by right and keep the boys at home? The protesters were convinced, and the gold rush of Australia was on—with Hargraves the new Commissioner of Crown Lands. Now it was a turnabout, with Americans flooding the big island to try their luck, but conditions were not exactly the same, because the gold of Australia was not dust so much as nuggets. Enormous nuggets were found, and made history. The biggest ever found weighed two hundred pounds. The story is that it was discovered in 1869 near Ballarat by two partners whose cart of supplies got stuck in a muddy road. There was a large rock in the way, and one of the men, digging it out, nicked it, showing the solid gold beneath the muddy coat.

They were afraid to let anyone else see it, and the road was not exactly deserted. So with great care they finished exhuming the boulder, hoisted it up, and with many a grunt deposited it among the provisions in their cart, then resumed their trek to Melbourne, where they had originally been bound. Before they got there the cart broke down, but somehow they got the load to their cabin, where they buried the nugget under the floor and, to make all look innocent, built a fire just over the place. The fire, they explained to any pleased passerby who dropped in to make himself comfortable, was just to welcome strangers. Thus, when at last they fixed up the cart and were ready to carry the fortune to Melbourne, they decided to name the nugget the Welcome Stranger. (Australian nuggets of unusual size were always given names.) The Welcome Stranger is probably the largest nugget ever found.

The trouble with many of the goldfields in Australia was the lack of water. Naturally, without water one can hardly go panning in the traditional manner, so the miners evolved a new method called *dry blowing,* which entailed the use of two pans rather than one, and they called them not pans, but dishes. Western Australia, though short of water, has plenty of wind, so these miners simply put their dry sample in one dish, lifted it reasonably high above the other, and poured out the mixture of sand and gold. The unfailing wind carried off the sand, while the heavy gold rattled down on the dish beneath. It was much like winnowing chaff out of grain. Just as miners in wetter lands evolved an improvement on water panning—the cradle—these Australian prospectors (or fossickers, as they called themselves) eventually invented the *shaker,* a vehicle that was first cousin to a wheelbarrow—or perhaps more like a giant saltcellar. The shaker necessitated the use of a two-man crew, one to shovel golden sand into it, the other to shake it and at the same time blow air through it with a pair of bellows. No matter what the method, wet or dry, more than 14 million ounces of gold were taken out of Australian ground in the most active period, 1892–1915, and that wasn't all the gold there, either. Some of the mines are still being worked, though not at the original frenetic pace.

The next gold rush was a mixed one, mixed because what was found there in Nevada, near Virginia City, was silver—so they thought—rather than gold. Never mind; silver was good too. But in fact there was gold as well, mixed in with the silver in considerable quantity; it was a gold-silver alloy exactly like the electrum of the ancient world. In *The Richest Place on Earth,* edited by Warren Hinckle and Frederic Hobbs, the story is told of Gold Cañon and Gold Hill and the Comstock Lode generally. For a long time the strike appeared to be nothing much because the real pay dirt was earth of a peculiar color, soft and friable. And it was there at Virginia City that gold mining at last came of age, because panning and cradling did not suffice; more sophisticated methods were to be adopted. As the mineral was extracted, whole rooms, or stopes, were emptied, but the surrounding rock gave way so easily that ordinary techniques were not enough to protect the diggers. Thus they learned to shore up the rooms with timber, and as the stope was emptied of pay dirt it was refilled with waste rock, which held up the walls and roof.

It took twenty years, from 1860 to 1880, to work out the Comstock Lode. The takings were $300 million, no comfort for people who in 1858 fell for a rumor and, with the motto "Pike's Peak or Bust!," traveled in thousands to the Colorado landmark, where they found no gold. Nearby, however, at Gregory Gulch not far from Denver, there was plenty of it. In fact, before the rushes took place there was lots of gold in lots of places in North America.

Nor is it all a matter of history and nothing more. It seems today that the old-time diggers of the rushes didn't get all the gold, but that is a story for our next chapter. We should first look at South Africa, and we ought to look at Siberia as well, since nobody is sure which of the two countries, South Africa or Russia, produces most of the new gold in the world nowadays. It is not easy to say because the Russians, as in so many other fields, aren't telling. Timothy Green in *The World of Gold Today* (1973) cautiously listed gold production only in the non-Communist countries. Indubitably the Republic of South Africa headed this list. In thousands of ounces, her figure in 1972 was 29,215. Canada came a long way behind, though she was second: Her production for the same year was 2,080, and the United States was only third with 1,475. In decreasing amounts to represent them came Australia, Ghana, the Philippines, and so on, but South Africa was way out ahead. Her production for that year was 76.9 percent of the world's new gold—always leaving out the Communist countries.

However, it is not necessary to leave them out completely, even if the best one can do is comment on their secretive habits. An article in *The New York Times* of April 16, 1979, does a fair job of this. From Ust-Nera, USSR, Craig R. Whitney wrote:

> If you could figure out how much gold the Russians produced in this northeast Siberian mining town, you would probably be thrown into jail for spying. So secret are the figures that the posters outside the mine headquarters do not say how many tons were produced in January and February—they just say, "Plan fulfilled."

It's cold there. Nobody would live in that part of Russia if it weren't for the gold. The only country that produces more of the metal than Russia is South Africa. A United States Bureau of Mines estimate placed the 1980 Russian output at 270 tons. Much of the gold is turned up by prospectors, who still work in the old way in the Soviet gold country. An official interviewed by Whitney, though typically cautious, said that the state sends teams of twenty to a hundred prospectors at a time into the mountains.

"They make salaries depending on how much gold they find," he said, "and the more they find the better. At a minimum each one makes 8,000 to 10,000 rubles a year." That is $12,000 to $15,000, a princely salary by Soviet standards.

When the interviewer suggested that a prospector who found a big nugget might be tempted to smuggle it away, the official declared that it was not in the psychology of their people to steal. Anyway, nobody ever got close to a chunk of genuine gold unless there were at least two others to watch him carefully. At last he conceded that thieves were jailed, saying, "The more they steal, the longer they get."

According to Mr. Whitney, the museum at Ust-Nera displays two large nuggets, each about the size of a man's fist. These nuggets are only facsimiles, because, as the museum director commented, they would be stolen if they were real.

"Siberia is in many ways a natural treasury of precious metals and energy resources," continued the reporter, "but not much of it stays in the region."

They are also given loans to build shelter and cabins. "It's against our law to live in tents in this climate," [the official] said, "and it's illegal for an individual to stake a claim on his own or just go out panning."

The Siberian miner's life is very different from the life of the miner in South Africa, even the white miner, and there are not very many examples any more of this species. There used to be plenty, however. Remember the African port where tradesmen mariners, in ancient days, put out their wares and departed to wait for the natives to bring gold in exchange? If the natives weren't happy with the trade goods they went away too, it will be recalled, and the whole thing was done all over again until both sides were satisfied and gold had changed hands. Well, that gold came from southern Africa, very likely, and a few thousand years later it might well have been tracked to its source when, after the big finds in North America and Australia had been publicized, a number of determined treasure hunters descended on the African continent and started looking for more. It was 1884. At first their progress was impeded by preconceived no-tions, picked up in the other places, of how the gold ought to look. They did not guess that the African metal, unlike that in the placer mines of their tradition, was held in the grip of strata (sometimes only one thin stratum) of conglomerate which, to make matters more difficult, was often far beneath the earth's surface. It had to be (a) found and (b) worked. Conglomerate, as the word implies, is a mixture of pebbles and sand and, sometimes, gold all clotted together. The material was water-laid after having been eroded eons ago from its mother rock; a solution of this and that in water fused it together until—what with the cement and the pressure of more strata laid down on top of it, all of it then ground by the earth's movement in earthquakes or volcanic activity—it became hard rock all over again. This gold-bearing conglomerate—or reef, as it is called in geology circles —was and is secondary to the veins, probably of quartz, from which the gold was derived. I almost said "originally derived," but who knows, in this never-stable planet, what is original and what is not? Gold-bearing material can go through a dozen metamorphoses before the gold is found and held in human hands, none the worse for its experiences.

Some of the reef outcropped and eroded, but its gold wasn't in the rich alluvial form that the prospectors were looking for. One had to be tenacious to carry on prospecting in these unfamiliar conditions, or as lucky as George Harrison, who in spite of his experience (he had been a prospector in Australia) wasn't even looking for gold in South Africa when he found an auriferous outcrop on Langlaagte Farm, which belonged to the widow Anna Oosthuizen. Langlaagte was in Witwatersrand—Whitewater Rand—which nowadays, for the sake of brevity, everyone calls simply the Rand. Harrison was a builder when he wasn't looking for gold, and that day, with a partner named George Walker, he was digging on Widow Oosthuizen's land, hoping to find suitable stone for a house she wanted to build. The men were trying to go fairly deep because the surface farmland was not good for the purpose, being weathered and friable. Imagine their surprise when they recognized gold-bearing rock turned up by their spades. In fact it was what is called the Main Reef that they had stumbled on, and it was just their luck that at that point the conglomerate bed, arched like an angry cat's back, was closest to the surface. A few miles away and it would have been buried too deep for a casual discovery such as Harrison's. But he had stumbled on it and he knew enough to suspect what it was, and to tell Walker. Very likely he did not throw his spade into the air with a glad cry, because it wasn't, obviously, the rich find placer miners were used to, but he was an experienced prospector, so he and his partner took some of the rock home. They crushed it—not a difficult task, considering its nature—and panned it in the time-honored manner, and there it was: gold.

"That is the essence of the South African gold mines," commented Timothy Green in his book.

No one picks up nuggets. There is an unfathomable body of low grade ore stretching in the wide arc from 40 miles to the east of Johannesburg to 90 miles west, then swinging down southwest into the Orange Free State. The gold-bearing reefs, laid down perhaps 2,000 million years ago, vary in thickness from one-tenth of an inch to 100 feet, but on the average are only 1 foot thick.

It is only in the Free State Geduld (Orange Free State) that the gold between the pebbles can actually be seen. "While most mines in South Africa boast only a quarter to half an ounce of gold per ton of ore," says Green, "and it requires a magnification of at least two times to see even the largest specks of gold, Free State Geduld has an average of nearly one ounce per ton, making it one of the richest gold mines in the world today."

At first the miners carried on their trade in the way that we might call Method Number Two, used after picking up placer gold from the surface of the earth: They chopped at the veins they saw, following them until they were lost, in the meantime grinding up the ore they recovered. But these were peculiar veins that led them every which way as they dived into the ground. A man's claim might seem very promising, but what good was it when the lode took sudden dips that led its worker straight down and under another man's lode? It was obvious from the beginning that no matter where you worked it, the pay dirt was on an awkward slope—and not always the same slope, either. It also became apparent very soon that this was big-time mining, not to be done on a shoestring. The deeper you went the more it cost to bring gold out, until the small man decided that it no longer paid at all to mine gold—not in South Africa, at any rate. He dropped out.

But waiting to take his place, and not always waiting, either, was the new phenomenon of South Africa, the diamond millionaire. These generals of industry—for one can hardly call them anything less, such as captains—had already made fortunes and had plenty of capital to sink into the auriferous ground on their doorstep. Rand Mines, Gold Fields, General Mining and Finance Corporation, Johannesburg Consolidated Investment, and Union Corporation were the first and, with two exceptions, the last to corner the market. The exceptions are Sir Ernest Oppenheimer's Anglo American, and Anglo-Vaal—formerly Anglo-Transvaal Consolidated Investment. The first five were settled in the gold industry before the turn of the century; Anglo American came in in 1917, Anglo-Vaal in 1933. Now all seven run things tidily. To quote Timothy Green yet again:

Although each individual mine is floated as a separate company, with its own shareholders, chairman, board of directors, and mine manager, its destiny is guided by one of these giant seven. They provide the financial security, administrative experience and technical know-how that a mine could not hope to develop alone.

It was as a guest of Anglo American that I first visited a gold mine in South Africa, and that was a long time ago, before Sir Ernest died. There was a dance being held that day by the black mine workers, who indulged in the pastime every Sunday. I remember quite a lot of talk about how some of the authorities thought the dances a good idea but others were against them in the interests of what they called detribalization: The sooner a miner forgot his tribal customs and settled down to work, these anti-anthropologist people told me, the better. I don't know if the argument was ever settled. I was more interested in the contours of the country around Johannesburg. What were those enormous hills that surrounded the city? They were the tailings from the mines, I was told, the unwanted rock, or gangue, that was combined with gold in natural ore and later discarded after crushing. Some of these tailing heaps were very old, and attempts had been made to beautify them by planting bushes and even trees as well as grass all over them. But as most of the tailings had gone through various processes—amalgamation with mercury in the old days, then the use of cyanide—it took I don't recall how many years for the cyanide to weather out before the soil was able to support vegetation. Then the price of gold went up, demand was high, and it was discovered that there was still a lot of gold in those hills, so the tailings were worked over again and again. South Africa is a restless place on that account.

There are many more South African gold mines than those I saw near Johannesburg. Of course there are mines all the way along the Reef, but the only one I saw was that one not far from the city, and I was very much impressed. It happens that I have been down lots of mines, but I have never, before or since, seen such a model of its kind. The elevator that took me down—no rickety bucket, but a proper working platform —felt safe, solid, and somehow established. When we got to the bottom of the workings I found myself among white-washed walls with ceilings of surprising height. Electric lights hung from the ceilings or shed their glow from side-wall brackets. I was correct in thinking the elevator established, because this mine had been dug years before and was clearly there to stay awhile. I was tenderly placed on a miniature streetcar and taken on a tour of inspection. We rode past more and more whitewashed walls, imperceptibly going down and down into the earth, until at last we came to a less or-derly part of the mine, where work was being done on the face; there was a smell of explosive in the air just before it was whisked out by their excellent ventilation system, and no-body had as yet whitewashed anywhere. Cars were in evi-dence, too, carrying lumps of dynamited ore toward the lifts or rumbling back for new loads. Outside the mine, I knew, these loads would be dumped into an enormous machine that ground them up, sorted out the gold, and pushed or carried everything by belt to its appointed destination. That was a long way off, yet even in the middle of all this careful, in-sulated, expensive development there was an overpowering noise in my ears, the grinding of ore at the face.

"What?" I had to yell at my escort.

He yelled back, "That water over there—look."

I looked and saw a steady fall of water, a stream like that coming out of a giant's tap, coming down the rock wall.

The escort shouted something about how deep in the ground

we were—about a mile and a half. "Go on over," he said, "and feel it. The water, I mean."

I obeyed. It was indeed like water out of a tap: a giant's bathwater. It was steaming, heated by terrestrial action, pure, original heat we mortals had nothing to do with. It gave me a strong feeling I can't quite explain, that I was in touch as never before with the elements.

"Ready?" asked the guide, gesturing toward the tramcar.

"Just a minute," I shouted. I turned back to the rock wall and felt the water again.

11

NUGGETS

At the beginning of the last chapter I said that we are familiar with the general story of the forty-niners, and it is true. Therefore it was with a sense of *déjà vu* that I read in a Sunday paper not so long ago that prospectors were at it again in the West, going out with their pans and, for all I knew, their mules. No, surely not mules—more likely jeeps full of provisions. Anyway there they were, looking for gold, which is again in short supply (there is more, far more, where it came from, but it needs getting out) because it is worth more than it ever has been, as far, at least, as we can remember. The seekers, it seemed, were panning all the way down from Alaska through Canada and into California and Nevada. A lot of them were making a picnic of it, which the old-timers didn't have the leisure or temperament for. Probably these so-called prospectors are just pot-smoking kids, I said to myself. But my attention was caught and tickled just the same, and I was glad to find an article in the *New York Times* of November 22, 1978, that discussed the trend. By Peter J. Schuyten, it started out, "Don't look now, but another gold rush may be on the way. With gold selling around $200 an ounce"—which dates the article to any goldwatcher; it is selling for lots more than that now—"the combination of new techniques and portable mining equipment is starting to make previously uneconomical gold deposits attractive to both small groups of miners and large mining companies alike."

Mr. Schuyten went on to say that thirty-five to forty small gold mines were being worked in several Western states: California, Wyoming, Colorado, and Montana. He described the mining that a small-scale operator can afford nowadays; light, easily portable machinery, such as a miniature grinding mill, makes it possible and profitable, *if* the price of gold stays up—above, say, $150 an ounce. But what interested me more was the thought of old mines being reactivated. History is often so final that one smells the stale air of the museum when reading it. (Not that I don't like museums, but they are for Sunday afternoon, not weekday living.) It is good when something happens to pump new life into old institutions. So I went to California in November 1978 and stayed with friends, a young couple who don't smoke pot and whose interest is not directly in gold but is not far away from it either. In their spare time—they are social workers during the week—they hunt minerals. I think they are called rock hounds or rock chasers, but rocks *qua* rocks are not really their object. What they like are crystal aggregates. Most of us have seen this sort of thing, most commonly formations of amethyst crystals lining the cavity of a hunk of other stone, or miniature landscapes in the openings made by cracks in limestone, reproductions of the interior of Mammoth Caves, with tiny stalagmites and stalactites. If we happened to visit the New York Museum of Natural History at the right time, we saw superb examples of these things, awesomely beautiful clusters of large, perfect quartz or sulfur crystals, bigger than doorstops, bigger even than cornerstones.

Well, these friends of mine, John and Janey, collect things like that, for their beauty, rarity, and general interest. Their house is full of mineral specimens, and their minds are stocked with strange technical knowledge and jaw-breaking chemical names. Through their so-called rocks the couple have a very good idea of the mineralogy of the mountains around San Mateo, where they live.

I was there because John had a friend who was interested in a gold mine. The news, so commonplace a generation ago, was sufficiently unusual today to give us a talking point that went on for a long time. The friend, John explained, did not want his mine publicized in any way. He feared a new gold rush, and perhaps a fate like John Sutter's.

"I don't know how much gold he hopes to get out of it," said John, "or whether it's of secondary interest, in his mind, to the little guesthouse he has started up. The inn is very attractive, furnished all through in nineteenth-century style—"

"Except for the plumbing," his wife interposed.

"Yes, of course, the plumbing's modern. I was going to suggest that we take you there to stay overnight, but the tourist season's at its height, and we couldn't get places. Anyway, as I understand it, you're not interested in plain, simple sightseeing."

I said he understood correctly. "I wanted to see genuine gold-mining," I added.

"Then my friend's place wouldn't be right for you anyway," John replied. "We found something in last Friday's paper that might interest all of us. Here it is." He handed me a copy of the *San Mateo Times* for September 22, 1978.

Under the headline NEW FEVER IN THE MOTHER LODE: BIG GOLD OPERATION SET TO START, the story, datelined San Francisco, ran:

A Canadian firm, eager to cash in on the record price of gold, is nearly ready to produce its first bars of the precious yellow stuff from the rocky ground of California's storied gold-rush country. The Blazing Star Mine is the name of their game, situated near tiny West Point, on the eastern tier of the Mother Lode, where the 1848 discovery transformed America. In ten roaring years, miners panned and tore $6 million of the soft yellow metal from the streams and hills. The State Division of Mines and Geology says the Blazing Star effort is the most ambitious and expensive in California today. With gold at over $200 an ounce, the Blazing Star's owner, Troy Gold Industries Limited of Calgary, Alberta, claims the mine has a potential to gross 7.5 million in gold the first year, plus several million more in by-product tungsten, copper, and silver. According to the state agency, 6,900 ounces of gold were mined in California last year. At an average of about $190 an ounce, that came to over $1.3 million. Troy Gold estimates the first year of production at 37,500 ounces and hopes to melt its first gold next month. State geologist Gary Taylor said there are fewer than half a dozen small mining operations throughout California. Most of the state's gold production, however, comes from sand and gravel operations, in which the gold washes out of the material, he said. James Farrell, president of Troy Gold, said more than $2 million has been spent so far to bring the 95-year-old Blazing Star to production. Farrell hired Thomas R. Tough's geology firm in Vancouver, B.C., to survey the mine. Their report states that samples removed from four of the mine's veins indicate at least 30,000 tons of minable ore, averaging more than an ounce per ton of ore. A check of areas below the value surveyed brings that figure up to 200,000 mineable tons, according to the New York-based Precious Metals Society.

Farrell, 52, said he hopes to push the mine down thousands of feet more to develop a 15-year supply of ore. Tough, who said he has no interest in Troy Gold or the Blazing Star, said in a telephoned interview that a sample from one vein tested out at a very rich twenty-six ounces of gold per ton. Another rated nineteen ounces. [These figures are freakishly high, by the way. Perhaps the reporter was mistaken in what he heard.] Farrell, whose company bought the mine two years ago in the belief that the world's currencies are going to hell, said he was surprised to discover the results of diamond-drilling tests showed the Blazing Star claim had already been mined down to the oxidized or free gold zone. To Farrell, this meant the early miners literally had barely scratched the surface of this Calaveras County mine.

To get to the gold, the raw ore must be milled, a process which involves pulverizing the ore, separating the gold, and refining it at the mine site. Some of the gold, tightly bonded to other compounds in the ore, must be chemically treated, and is shipped to a smelter. The Blazing Star is an unusual departure from the traditional shaft mines of the Mother Lode. It is called a spiraling decline, descending over a 1,600-foot length into the ground like a corkscrew, down to about 400 feet. The slope is wide enough to accommodate vehicles, including front-end loaders which carry the ore. There is room for the vehicles to turn around, and where two vehicles meet head on, one can move into a turn-out to allow the other to pass.

The mine is a combination of several veins, with the creative names Last Chance, Never Sweat, Matrimony, and Blazing Star. The biggest gold mine in the United States is the 7,000-foot-deep Homestake Mine, at Lead, South Dakota, which produced over 300,000 ounces of gold last year. The mine has been producing for more than a century. Russell Wallace, vice president of Marketing, said the Homestake ore assays at between a fifth and a third of an ounce of gold per ton.

"First I thought of telephoning to see if visitors are allowed," said John, "but I didn't have the number and it's complicated when you aren't in the neighborhood. It's a nice drive, so I thought we might as well try our luck. I figure as it's a weekend they might not be working, in which case they won't be so touchy about letting us look around. We'll find a motel somewhere in the vicinity for the night—it's half a day's drive at least, so let's get started."

We loaded the car and set off. Soon we left orderly, civilized San Mateo and got deeper and deeper into genuine California countryside, which might best be described as tamed but not cowering. Here and there we saw a dirt road. Some houses had avenues of walnut trees and looked rather elegant in an English way, but they had none of the snooty splendor of certain estates in Virginia. Others were shacks, pleasant enough and tidily painted, but shacks all the same. But mostly there were no houses, just wooded hillsides and tangled brush. Whenever we came to a town, John looked for certain signs: ROCKS, or ROCKS SOLD. Some of these, he explained, he knew of old; others were new and would bear investigation.

"Goodness," I said. "I had no idea so many people were keen on collecting. If I weren't with you I might not have noticed those signs at all, but now that I've seen them—why, there are lots of them."

Janey said, "Oh, there are. We have clubs, you know. Some people own territory that's good for hunting specimens, and so many people have begun swarming in that a lot of the landowners have slammed a charge on the privilege. I guess it becomes a nuisance, lots of people crawling around with hammers."

"I didn't know," I replied humbly. I am often humbled by the thought of the many life-styles I know nothing about.

As we drew near our goal the landscape became more rugged, with outcrops of red soil hanging over the road where it had been cut out. We passed a signpost telling us we were getting near Sutter's Mill, and as we drove through the valley indicated we saw the mill itself, or so it seemed to me. Apocryphal? Because, after all, he never finished it.

"There's a museum there," John told me, "and some of the tools of the old-time prospector, if you're keen enough to spend the time, but I think we'd better be getting along."

These were steep little hills we were driving through, I noted —little hills on the sides and tops of mountains. Probably they had been dug into, tested, and plundered or foresaken a hundred years ago. At a crossroads garnished by a filling station and a general store we paused for directions from an Indian boy in Levi's, crossed over and mounted a little rise, and were confronted by a large new sign:

BLAZING STAR MINE
TROY GOLD INDUSTRIES LTD.

It was to one side of a gate, high and closed, in a tall fence that did not hide the land beyond. Muttering, "I suppose it's locked," John honked his horn, and a man soon appeared within the compound on his way to the gate. We had our little speech all prepared, but he was not hard to persuade. The gate swung open.

"You see those two trailers up there," he said, gesturing. "Go to the furthest one and ask for Mr. Farrell."

In the trailer, comfortably fitted out like a business office, a youthful-looking man telephoned to find Mr. Farrell. In the meantime, he said, we could sit down and ask questions. He was very forthcoming. He too was from Canada, but he didn't know much about mining yet; he was learning, as assistant to Mr. Farrell. Oh, yes, lots of people were dropping by to look at the workings. There had been all that publicity. There's something about gold, he said, and we agreed; yes, there certainly is. He had embarked on telling us how many sightseeing parties they had shown around that day, Saturday, when Mr. Farrell came in.

A rather small, thin man, Mr. Farrell was engagingly open and enthusiastic about his mine. I wondered, after a few minutes, why we had ever doubted our welcome. It was obvious that he wanted to talk and also to show us more of the printed publicity that accompanied his project. Let it speak for him:

"Farrell, the man behind the reopening of the Blazing Star Mine," said an article in a throwaway called the *Troy Gold Transcript,* printed to look like a paper of a hundred years ago, complete with old illustrations and advertisements,

is the real thing, a prospector shaped by the dangerous drudgery of hardrock mining rather than the imaginative fancies of Madison Avenue image makers. The 52-year-old Farrell, a native of Vancouver, British Columbia, is the chief executive officer of Troy Gold Industries Ltd. of Calgary, Canada. . . . The gold bug first bit Farrell when he was 18 years old. At that time he was a hand mucker in the Pioneer Gold Mine in the Bridge River Valley of British Columbia. [A hand mucker is a man who shovels ore and gangue in a mine.] He no longer is hand mucking, but he's still scratching the itch that he got from that bug 34 years ago.

Since then he's been chasing the rainbow—and frequently finding the pot of gold at the end—as a miner's helper, chuck tender, stope miner, drift miner, mine operator and mine owner. He organized Troy Gold Industries Ltd., which takes its name from the town of Troy in the northwest corner of Montana rather than from the traditional weight measurement of gold, in 1974. He acquired the Blazing Star in 1975 for $600,000.

Mr. Farrell went on talking, saying essentially the same thing the article did—perhaps he wrote it, I thought irreverently—but there was nothing tired about what he said. He enjoyed his mine; he loved it. Not long before, they had poured out the first gold brick from the metal taken out of the Blazing Star; it now reposed in a bank vault, where it would shortly, he hoped, be joined by a twin. He showed us a plan of the corkscrew vein and pointed out that its strange shape was really advantageous in that one didn't need as much surface area as other, more wandering veins called for. They had resumed work two years earlier digging it out, finding that the ramp went down four hundred feet vertically—at least so far at a 20 percent decline. This obviously made it easier to mine than if the vein had been as steep as most of the others not far away.

"We've got five veins of pay dirt," said Mr. Farrell, "and we've intercepted the Blazing Star vein four times so far with our ramp. Now, though it's still too early to tell, we've got an idea that one of the other veins runs into the Blazing Star; we expect to find out in a few days. Of course that ought to enrich the vein even more. That mill over there"—indicating a large structure between the trailers and the fence—"cost the company seven hundred thousand dollars, and it looks as if it'll be worth every dollar. It's got a jaw crusher, a cone crusher, and a ball mill. The gold is in quartz, of course, like most of the gold around here; we run the ore when it's been pulverized over blanket tables, flotation cells, and riffle tables. I'll show you all that later. At the moment we process about seventy-five tons a day, but when we're working full out, seven days a week, on day and night shifts, we can do a hundred and fifty. It's not working, but you might like to look at the mill and, on the way, our new little assay office. It's been assaying at two or three ounces of gold per ton; on some days they come up with nineteen ounces, but I don't intend to believe it's really that rich."

"Surely two or three ounces is pretty rich, even so?" I said, timidly.

"Oh, yes," he said cheerfully. "We aren't banking on three, but two is possible. At any rate, our calculations are based on one ounce. That way we won't come out on the wrong side. Even so it's a lot more than the percentage they get in Canada's top ten gold mines—point thirty-two ounce per ton."

"And South Africa?" asked John.

"About half an ounce," said Farrell.

"But if the vein's that rich, why did they suspend operations a century ago?"

Farrell beamed. "Because all they cared about was the weathered quartz. They were familiar with that kind of mining, you see; rotten rock and gold already weathered out. The minute they came to the hard stuff they thought they were in trouble. It wasn't only that they had to crush the ore; chemically it wasn't feasible. I've been reading the old records, and there's a lot in them about 'sulfurets.' Every so often you come across the word: 'We hit sulfurets so we didn't go any deeper.' "

Sulfurets? As soon as I got the chance I looked them up in Gina Allen's book, the reference work that had the most to say about Western America's gold mines. She didn't mention Blazing Star, but she did speak at length of a Colorado region, the aforementioned Gregory Gulch, where a lode of ore was called "blossom rock," the "crumbly quartz outcrop of an underground vein of gold," so much weathered that it was easy to crush and sluice it. It was very rich. "No man digging in the area made less than one hundred dollars a day." This, I need hardly say, was back in the days of the gold rush, which was at its most rushing just then at Gregory Gulch. The miners followed the auriferous rock—but let Gina Allan tell it.

They followed the rich blossom rock farther and farther into the mountain. . . . Gold mining in Gregory Gulch took on all the aspects of a permanent industry. And then, suddenly, the blossom rock turned rebellious. It refused to yield its gold.

What had happened was that the gold in its uneroded state had formed an alloy with iron, which was combined with sulfur as iron pyrite, and nobody could figure out a way to extract it. They ground it down, but still the gold clung chemically to the iron. Only about a tenth of it was recovered. In the ordinary way the miners would have tried the mercury route, running the ground-down ore over mercury with which it immediately bonded as amalgam; then the amalgam was heated and the mercury evaporated. Presto! You had gold. But with this alloy the gold refused to let go of the sulfides, which counteracted the effect of the mercury. These ores, therefore, were called sulphurets, or sulfurets; and the original owners of Blazing Star, like those of Gregory Gulch, simply packed it in and went away. A good thing for Mr. Farrell, he obviously thought.

John tentatively mentioned that we would like to see the mine. He was tentative because he had already experienced caution among others of the new breed of mine owners; if Mr. Farrell had made excuses we would have understood perfectly. But Mr. Farrell didn't.

"Of course you can see it," he said heartily, "though naturally it isn't in the best condition. We've had to pump water out of it, especially after all this wet weather, but it's quite feasible to go down. We aren't working it today except for a little tidying up at the face. Come along."

Around on the other side of the mill we went down a flight of steps into an office where he fitted each of us out with a miner's cap complete with headlight and a battery in a kind of backpack. ("It's the law," he said apologetically. "Nobody can go down without one of these hats.") We also had to have boots, but when it came to putting on a pair of the mine's rubber boots I protested.

"These I'm wearing are waterproof," I said. "They fit better than those, too."

Mr. Farrell did not insist. So, hatted and booted, we followed him down a rocky path to the mine entrance. If the path outside was rocky it was nothing compared to the state of the ground underfoot once we were out of the sun, with our miners' hats lit up. I barely had time to reflect that this mine was not in the least like the one I had visited in South Africa. There was no time for reflection; all my attention was devoted to staying upright. Rocks rolled underfoot or impeded my steps; worse, they were very wet rocks. At times the pathway was a running stream. On either hand were the walls, gleaming in the lamps' rays like the sides of demon caves. I went so slowly—because I couldn't go faster—that Janey put her arm under mine and helped me over the many bad bits. This was humiliating; worse, I had been wrong (or the man who sold them to me had been wrong) about my boots, which were not in the least waterproof.

Still, even as I squelched and stumbled along, I was fascinated. Through these same walls the early miners had worked; indeed, they had excavated them. This very corridor, narrow and high, had carried the Blazing Star vein which led them deeper and deeper into the earth. Now and then on the floor, among the rocks, I saw tracks along which the ore wagons had passed with their load.

"We're at about three hundred feet now," Mr. Farrell was telling us. "Here's a crosscut." Even darker in the gloom, two subsidiary corridors disappeared in the distance. We were making, he told us, for the mine face—the new workings—where, they hoped, two rich veins were coming together.

The mine was not quite deserted. Along the way we picked up a rubber-booted man carrying a pick, and soon afterward came a rumble and then a kind of platform on wheels driven by a third man, who was going to fetch a load, we were told, just to fill in the time. Now the rubble looked fresher, and I saw John pick up a flat rock—a piece that exhibited a good hunk of gold, no doubt. He put it into his knapsack.

Things got wetter and wetter. It was raining in the mine, and Mr. Farrell directed one of his helpers to apply the pump to a particularly deep-looking puddle.

I said, "I think I saw a crocodile there on the other side."

"It does look eerie in the lamplight," said Mr. Farrell, laughing. "We're nearly there."

And there we were, indeed, in a widening of the corridor, almost a room. Across the end of it was the living rock, the face. Mr. Farrell said, "One doesn't see the vein well unless it's wet." He directed one of his aides to throw a bucket of water over it, and for just a minute we saw the vein, or rather two veins, clearly against the surrounding rock. They did run together, forming a thick-looking V, and before the water ran off we could see, here and there, a tiny sparkle.

Going back didn't take as long. It never does.

Waiting for tea in Mr. Farrell's trailer, the other one with a much more homelike interior, we talked in low tones, as he busied himself in the kitchen, about what seemed to us his extraordinarily frank approach. John, who was used to cautious mine owners, was particularly puzzled.

"Announcing in the papers that they're going to pour another gold bar," he said. "Isn't that asking for trouble?"

Janey wasn't so sure. "They're bound to see that they're well protected," she said, "and they're doing it right there at the bank, aren't they? Where the vault is?"

"Yes." John was still dubious. "But I must say he doesn't seem at all keen on selling shares or anything. I'm not sure I wouldn't want to invest a bit if they had it right there on the market, but I don't think it's listed."

No, said Mr. Farrell cheerfully as he came back with the tea tray. They hadn't listed the shares. There was no need to; they were already capitalized all they wanted, at least for the time being. Later on, of course, they would see. As for secrecy, he handed out a lot more literature before we left and said we could come back any time, any time. Later, in the car, I read one of the papers I clutched. Published in New York, it said in part, "Troy Gold Industries Ltd. . . . An interesting situation which is well-positioned to benefit from the current price-rise of gold is TROY GOLD INDUSTRIES LTD., a Calgary (Canada) -based mining company organized in 1974 and, since April 1976, listed on the Alberta Stock Exchange."

"Well, it's listed in Canada anyway," I said, interrupting my reading. "It says here that they've been working a mine in Montana called the Morning Glory, as well as here."

The article continued, after a paragraph or two on the Morning Glory:

A more immediately productive property of TROY GOLD's is closer to home: the *Blazing Star* complex in California's Sierra Nevada mountain range, in the heart of the legendary "Mother Lode" of Gold Rush fame, 55 miles east of Sacramento. (The "Mother Lode," a 120-mile-long belt flanking the Sierra Nevadas, is known to be rich in gold-bearing quartz-sulfide and appears to be anything but mined out. According to a 1975 report by the U.S. Bureau of Mines, the area "is believed to represent a very large resource of gold . . . probably the second-largest domestic resource . . . with undiscovered resources remaining to be found in relatively small but possibly rich 'bonanza' lode deposits.")

"It certainly sounds all right," said Janey, when I finished reading aloud, and John agreed.

We found a motel not far away from the filling station and took rooms there. It was a new building, very utilitarian but also very clean. We asked the owner (who had to be called from the filling station with the key to the rooms) what he had to say about the Blazing Star.

"Well, folks around here like the people and the mine," he replied readily. "It's brought work to the neighborhood, and we needed that. Yes, sir, we needed it."

Next day on the way back we stopped at a nearby town for something to eat. A lot of it has been rebuilt in the style of the 1850s; the sidewalks, all up and down, run past store windows that reproduce as nearly as possible the windows that must have attracted the miners of those days. John said, "There used to be a very good rock store on the next block. . . . Yes, there it is. Janey, shall we have a look?"

Inside the shop were counters full of souvenirs, not too bad, and a few rocks that according to John were not bad at all. There were also samples of rich gold-bearing ore. The woman who owned the place recognized my friends, and a long conversation about the Blazing Star followed. Yes, she said, she was sure it was genuine, and if it was, it meant a lot to all the towns around. Already people were getting jobs at the mine and secondary ones outside as a result of it.

We drove away, down a hill that was steeper, it seemed to me, than any of San Francisco's most terrifying streets. All around us were tourists and quaint rebuilt hotels and boardinghouses. In my nostrils was a smell I associate with mines no matter where I am in the world, a dusty, parched smell that seems to go with red-yellow earth where grass never gets a chance to grow. It was just about the only genuine thing in that district, I reflected—the smell and, of course, the Blazing Star. (Because by that time, of course, I was a passionate adherent of the Blazing Star, which is proving itself very profitable. The latest time I checked up, about the middle of March 1980, there was a lot of activity in the country farther north of the mine, with old-fashioned prospectors swarming over the mountain rivers with their picks and pans and even burros. There is talk of gunplay over promising claims, and the place is getting crowded, but the Blazing Star, serene in the knowledge that it is firmly entrenched, remains peaceful.)

On further reflection, I had to include my friends and the other members of their rock-hunting fraternity, but most of all I thought of the dusty, earthen smell and what it brought to mind, which was, in a word, Welkom. It was in Welkom, a South African town built completely out of the gold-mining industry, that I saw my first and only gold bar being poured, and I'll never forget it.

The preliminaries were elaborate and, like so many other South African activities, haunted by the necessity of security. Guards stood outside the laboratory doors and other guards were inside, each at his appointed place near the machinery out of which the gold would come. A PR man stood at my elbow telling me what was going on inside that wizard's construction, what temperature was needed to melt the gold down, what chemicals had to go into the molten mass to purify it to the requisite percentage—ninety-nine point something pure gold. The men busying themselves around the magic tap were wearing masks, protective glasses, long asbestos (I think it was asbestos) gloves, and other protective clothing such as aprons. They carried tongs. A utensil rather like a deep bread-baking pan stood waiting. Then came the gold.

It came not like the shower of gold that descended on Danaë, but as a simple, slow flow, straight from the pages of John Ruskin's *The King of the Golden River,* save that it was obviously very hot indeed. It was a beautiful reddish-gold color, more red than gold when it first came out of the channel. It filled the bread-baking pan almost to the brim, and then, very neatly, it stopped. The bread did not rise, but lay there smoking, with the smoke slowly decreasing as the red faded. Somebody squirted cold water on it, and it hissed and smoked some more and faded yet more. One had to be patient. In the end there it was, a gold bar, stamped on the underside with the sign of legality and purity. It was very beautiful. I suppose I ought to remember what it was worth on the world market, but it doesn't really matter because it would be worth much more today; its value during that long-ago moment in Welkom has passed into history. But the parched smell of miner's earth, and its dusty, worked-over look, is still the same.

12

STICKPINS

From my Webster's *New Collegiate Dictionary:* "**carat** (. . . fr. Gk. *keration,* little horn, carob bean . . .) abbr. *c.* 1. A unit of weight for precious stones. . . . 2. A twenty-fourth part:—used to express the fineness of a gold alloy: as, 14 *carats* fine, i.e., being 14 parts gold and 10 alloy."

It seems pure nitwittery to use the same word to qualify two such different substances, especially when the substances, gold and gems, are often combined, in our thoughts and in reality, as for example a diamond and gold ring, a gold watch set with rubies or emeralds, or a jeweled crown of gold. No wonder people get the two measurements confused. The newer dictionaries distinguish between these usages by employing different spellings for the word, such as *karat* or *karet* for—well, for either gold or gems, but of course I cannot recall which; the confusion is too firmly planted in my head. Clearly it is not a cure for the situation, not even a mitigation. One's simply got to get used to it, that's all.

"This is fourteen-carat gold," said Bill Landau of Marsha Breslow, Designer. He handed me a small glass container with bits of metal in it. His brother-in-law, Alan Breslow, added, "Those are called casting grains."

I stared at the shining little fragments. They could have been discarded tooth fillings, I reflected, or chippings from Australian nuggets, or pieces of necklaces or bracelets from ancient Egyptian tombs, or agglomerated gold dust from the Homestake Mine, or drops of meltings from Scythian loot. Or they could have

represented all these sources and more; it was distinctly possible
that gold from some, at least, were contained in that little lot.
Gold may be, and is, used over and over. From time to time it
is alloyed or contaminated; then it is purified and starts all over
again. These castings were to be incorporated into medium-
priced jewelry, *new* jewelry, for American women.

We were sitting at a worktable in the middle of the main room.
It is large, with a lot of equipment that I didn't recognize in one
alcove, and many entrances and exits. Marsha is not only the
designer, she is Alan's wife and Bill's sister, but that day she was
working in another office. The establishment takes up the whole
floor of a building on West 39th Street in New York. One goes
through a whole lot of what is called Security to get into it:
metal-shuttered windows for those inside to look out of, bells
with red handles to sound alarms if necessary, locks and bolts to
be opened after there has been a careful inspection—all the
precautions that come naturally to people who do business in
gold and gems. Bill had promised to show me the mysteries of
casting and had chosen as a typical example the production of a
kind of gold stickpin that was in demand that year as a fashion
item. Marsha had designed a pin without jewels, a symmetrical
golden rosette to be stuck into a coat lapel or a scarf. I was assured
that it was a simple ornament, a simple job.

Alan introduced a small, powerful, dark-skinned man named
Ramiro, who smiled politely but clearly did not understand what
was being said.

"Ramiro does most of the actual work," said Alan. "He's from
Colombia, where there are a lot of goldsmiths. His father was a
goldsmith too. He already knew a lot when he came here, and
we've trained him to use whatever equipment wasn't familiar to
him before he joined us, and now he's very useful."

With Bill I moved over to the table with the mysterious gadg-
ets, and Ramiro, who had everything laid out in readiness for his
exposition, got busy at once. First I was shown the gold stickpin
that he was to reproduce. Then I was handed, to feel, a piece of
hard black material that had a little flexibility. Bill told me it was
rubber.

"Compressed rubber," he added, "and it's good for carving. A
whole lot of layers have gone into it. That block of rubber Ramiro

is holding"—Ramiro obligingly held it up for me to look at—"is ready for work. Here."

He took the block and showed that it had been cut in half. In the exact center of the rectangle, on each side, was the impression of Marsha's stickpin, so that the two halves put together would make an empty hole just the size and shape of the model. In other words, each half was an intaglio. At each large end was a small channel for letting in wax—for I was about to witness an example of the ancient lost-wax, or *cire-perdue,* process of casting. Ramiro had carved the mold, Bill explained, a job at which he excelled. I watched the goldsmith inspect the two halves very carefully, blowing into one of them to remove something that was invisible to me. Bill said, "The mold's got to be absolutely clean before he starts injecting the wax. Even a little grain of sand or whatever can ruin the product."

Later I got hold of a textbook called *Centrifugal Casting as a Jewelry Process,* by Mickey Story (Scranton, Pa., 1963), and learned the details of what I had seen. In it I learned that the right plastic, claylike working quality in wax can be attained by heating it to a temperature that will soften without melting it. One can put it directly below an infrared lamp to get this consistency, or immerse it in warm (not hot) water for a short time. Very hard wax can be carved almost like wood. There are of course various sorts of wax; the kind recommended by Mr. Story is a mix of beeswax and paraffin, but a lot depends on what kind of work the jeweler is going to cast. There is a wide variety on the market.

Bill showed me a rubber block similar to the one we were looking at, clamped together and in place in a machine that reminded me a bit of a kitchen blender, except that it was silent. This, he said, was the wax injector, with the power to force the melted wax into the cavity. It needed plenty of power to make sure the cavity was properly filled, all detail covered so that no holes could be left because of air bubbles or other extraneous causes. We didn't have to wait for injection to be completed, however; Ramiro had a model already made to show me—a waxen stickpin complete in every detail. He must have been making replicas of his model for some time, because a number of them were ready for casting, stuck into a ball about three inches in diameter, like so many porcupine quills, or cloves in an apple. The base on which they stood was also of wax, surrounded by a thick rubber pad.

"Now it's ready to be cast," said Bill. We adjourned to a neighboring room, where Ramiro handed Bill a steel cylinder of the same diameter as the base—the flask, Bill told me. It was fitted over the mold, then set aside, and Bill turned our attention to a kind of sink in the corner, with a bowl in it. He pointed to a sack of flourlike substance, saying, "This is the investment. It's something like plaster of Paris, and as it ought to stand for at least an hour before we use it, I've already mixed up some of it with water in that bowl. It's just about ready now."

Ramiro was fiddling with the model, and I saw that he had made a kind of wax spiral at the bottom of it.

"Ah," I said, proud that I had done homework. "That's the sprue, isn't it?"

Ramiro laughed, showing gold teeth, and nodded.

"That's it, for the wax to melt out in," said Bill. "Now we pour the investment."

He filled the flask halfway and let it stand for a bit, then filled it completely. "I couldn't show you the whole thing; there wasn't time in one day," he said. "The investment had to be jiggled before we used it, to avoid—"

"I know. Air bubbles!"

"Exactly. Anyway, it was vibrated for a certain amount of time, so we knew it was okay. Now the flask goes into the kiln. We're proud of this kiln; it's new."

It was also very large, I reflected, as Bill opened a white door and placed the flask carefully on a middle shelf, just as one might do with a frozen TV dinner. He shut the door, set a thermostat, and turned away.

"This kiln heats up from zero to thirteen hundred five degrees," he said, "but it must go at a steady increase, no sudden changes. The flask stays in there undisturbed for at least seven hours; usually we give it twelve, just to be safe. You have to count on two extra hours for what's called the burnout—that's when the wax evaporates and hardens the investment. In the meantime we make the gold ready here—" he crossed the room—"in the centrifugal casting machine."

The machine reminded me vaguely of a record player, because

it had an arm, but there wasn't much resemblance really. Bill explained certain facts about it, which will be more clear if I quote from Story's textbook:

The centrifugal casting machine is an apparatus which causes the arm holding the metal and the mold to revolve at a rate of approximately 300 revolutions per minute, forcing the metal into the mold by centrifugal force. It is important that the machine be carefully mounted so that it is perfectly level and free from vibration when in use.

What followed was complicated. A crucible, like a cup, was prepared, as described by Story:

The refractory crucible which will hold the molten metal may be lined with asbestos to aid in the melting of the metal and to prevent the metal from picking up foreign particles. Asbestos is cut to fit the floor of the crucible, moistened, and molded into place. . . . The casting machine must be wound in preparation for casting. The arm assembly should be given two and one-half to four complete turns. The arm is then locked into place with the stop rod. . . .

After the flask reaches the desired temperature for casting, the metal is melted in the crucible. A gas torch is used to melt the metal. The metal must not be overheated.

Bill poured the golden casting grains into his crucible and added several ingredients, to clean it, he explained. Then he put the cup into place and directed the blowtorch at it; it quickly melted. "The metal should appear shiny on the surface and should move easily if the arm of the machine is shaken gently," said the book. "However, it should never spit or boil." It did move easily; it glowed with a red-hot glow like the gold bar I had seen cast at Welkom. But this was a more elaborate kind of casting.

Bill, wearing an asbestos glove, now arranged a pre-baked flask against the crucible, to quote the book yet again,

so that the hole in the crucible is in alignment with the sprue through which molten metal will enter the mold cavity. With the flask in position, heat should once again be concentrated on the metal to ascertain that it has reached the proper liquid state. . . . Simultaneously the torch should be removed and the arm released, setting the machine in motion. The machine will continue to spin for two to five minutes. It should be allowed to spin until it stops naturally.

The thought crossed my mind, as I read, that this sounded too sophisticated to be used by the Scythians and all those other ancient people who cast their gold objects. Of course the thought was correct: Centrifugal casting has been in use only since just before the beginning of our century. In older days goldsmiths did without the elaborate machinery I saw at the Breslows', and probably managed quite well, except for the occasional air bubble or stopped-up sprue. But the machine makes it easier, not only for jewelers but dentists, who were the first to employ the method and, one supposes, could not do without it now.

The flask was allowed to cool off; not completely, however. Ramiro then plunged it into a bucket of cool water, and the investment plaster suddenly cracked off in a thousand pieces, leaving behind a little ball of golden stickpins where there had been wax stickpins before. It was magic. I think he was pleased by my surprise. He took his batch of new pins to his worktable, where he removed the plaster that remained here and there, chipping it off—a delicate operation, but not so delicate as the job that followed, examining each pin carefully for the most minute flaws. Some had run a little at the seams and had to be filed. Now and then he found a pin faulty enough, in his estimation, to discard; he put it aside to be added to other pieces of gold rejects. Even among the satisfactory pins there were occasional tiny crevices which he filled with gold solder, smoothing it over with a heated tool.

Bill observed my somewhat anxious look as the goldsmith discarded a pin. "It gets used again, don't worry," he said, kindly. "We often rework gold scraps. In fact we buy scrap as well as the grains you saw, but we have to be sure before we use it that it's up to standard, the right caratage and all that. Before we use it, it's got to be assayed and corrected where correction's needed."

There is, of course, much more to goldsmithing than the simple exercises this firm was kind enough to demonstrate. To get an idea of what is a vast subject, I referred to a primer for gold workers entitled *The Goldsmith's and Silversmith's Handbook* by Staton Abbey, published in 1952. I knew I need not worry that it was out of date; it wasn't. These things don't change much. From the *Handbook* I learned a number of facts, such as that gold used nowadays for jewelry making comes in four caratages: nine, fourteen, eighteen, and twenty-two. (Twenty-four carat gold is too soft to be used for many objects because it bends, rubs off, or is otherwise unsatisfactory. In Japan somewhere, I am told, there is a bathtub made of twenty-four-carat gold, for the benefit of people who want to say they have bathed in a twenty-four-carat golden bathtub. I don't want to carp, but according to the illustration of this marvel it is merely a hip bath, not the kind you can stretch out in, and I consider this cheese-paring.)

The *Handbook* told me that there is also a choice of more than fifty colors of gold, depending on certain factors including the temperature and the speed at which the molten metal is cooled, but mainly on alloys. The list of tints is tempting, like that of flavors at Baskin-Robbins. You can buy twenty-two-carat red, eighteen-carat yellow—a lot of yellows, in fact, ranging from very dark to very pale—Medium red, French green, hard white, soft white, plain green, and many more. Staton Abbey did not mention, because it had probably not yet been concocted, the black or near-black purple gold I saw recently at an exhibition of modern jewelry. The designer of this particular number told me that she had used malachite to achieve that tint. As the master goldsmith Fabergé discovered, yellow gold banded with green can be very effective, and so can a blended pattern of red with several yellows. The alloys give the different golds different qualities. Some are particularly good for enameling, and some won't hold the enamel at all. Some take kindly to spinning, or whirling on a rotating spindle while the gold is buffed into a soft gleam; this process doesn't work with others. Some are easily stamped, others not. Some, like the bits of fourteen-carat gold I saw at the Breslow studio, are fine for casting work.

Because the *Handbook* mentioned *drawing* so often, I looked it up from the index and learned that it is the process by which gold wire is made. As this wire is used a good deal in goldsmithing, its manufacture is important. Why gold wire? Because it was and is used in granulation, in which tiny balls of gold are affixed to a background of the smooth metal, for filigree work, and a dozen other things. One of the facts about gold that knowledgeable people love to impart is that it is so cohesive and ductile that if the smith starts out with a lump of it and begins to beat it, it can be spread thinner and thinner until it covers an incredibly large area. In fact, that is how gold leaf is made. The manufacture of wire is no less surprising. Before the sixteenth century goldsmiths had to hammer it out hour after hour on their anvils, but then some genius thought up the drawplate, and a goldsmith named Christopher Schultz, a Saxon who lived in France, introduced it into England about the middle of the century. The drawplate is a flat piece of steel about ten inches long with a row of holes, usually twenty, of graduated diameters drilled in a row. The largest hole is fairly coarse, the smallest fairly fine, and when you have reached the smallest hole in the plate, you may go on to another plate with even smaller holes drilled in it.

"In the workshop," continues Staton Abbey,

one end of the gold mass must first be tapered, either by rolling or by filing, to allow it to pass through the appropriate hole in the plate. The wire is then drawn through by winding it on to a drum. When the end of the wire has passed through the draw-plate, the whole coil is carefully removed from the drum (which is made slightly conical in form to facilitate removal) and placed upon a skeleton frame; it is then in proper form for its passage through the next hole of the draw-plate. In the production of very fine wire, the metal after passing a few times through the draw-plate requires annealing [that is, softening with heat and cooling to restore pliability] as it becomes hardened.

When gold has been overworked like this it becomes brittle because its crystals have been crushed and distorted. It must be persuaded to recrystallize—that is, form new crystals to replace the distorted ones, and this is done by heating.

I am also beholden to the *Handbook* for information on the refining of gold bullion. It seems that for jewelry making the customary percentages of purity are not enough; even 90 percent pure gold is not fine enough for some of the work done in studios. Chlorination is the answer. The bullion is melted and chlorine is passed through the mass until silver and the base metals that are still there have formed chlorides, which rise to the top of the broth and can be skimmed off. The remaining gold is 99.6 or 99.7 percent pure, but an even higher degree of purity can be achieved by dissolving the gold in aqua regia (a mixture of nitric and hydrochloric acids that dissolves gold), which is the only agent capable of performing in this way. Ferrous chloride is introduced, which precipitates gold that is ninety-nine and ninety-nine hundredths per cent pure. Few jewelers are pernickety enough to demand such a high standard.

In the lore of gold are many descriptions of the *cire-perdue* process of casting gold which I witnessed at the Breslow studio. After all, it is one of the oldest techniques in goldsmithing and was known all over the world in one form or another, in Siberia and the Near East as well as in America. Nevertheless it pleased me to find a highly comprehensible account of it in Benvenuto Cellini's *Treatises on Goldsmithing and Sculpture,* because it did not differ all that much from what Bill Landau and Ramiro demonstrated on that twentieth-century day in New York. Of course Cellini had no scientific devices to tell him the temperature of the furnaces, no electronic tools, and no centrifugally operated crucible. But he had a number of deft-handed assistants who would have understood thoroughly what Ramiro was doing, and the theory and method were in essence those of West 39th Street. This is how he described making a mold of a seal, an art form at which he excelled. It was a silver seal, not a gold one, but the procedure does not vary on that account.

He wrote:

But pay the greatest possible attention to what I am going to tell you now. Make a waxen form, almond-shaped, and of the exact size your seal is to be, hollow it out, and lay it over the surface of your gesso relief. [Gesso is plaster of Paris, which at that time took the place of hard rubber.] Then make your little ramparts of earth about this wax, taking heed to make due provision for the channel of the casting, which should be of ample length; & here I ought to tell you that the longer your channel is the better chance your work has of turning out well. There are no end of little details still to be observed, but if I were to tell you all of them I might as well begin teaching you your A B C. So I assume that my readers are people who have mastered the first principles of the Art. I would remind you, too, that both the ingress mouth & the vents have to be made of wax, & applied to the wax core. These vents are fixed below, & turn up around the seal towards the ingress mouth; they must not, however, come in contact with the latter, because they have to do their own work of drawing out the air. This done, bind up your seal with well tempered iron or copper wire, and let it bide in the sun, or some place where it can get warm & well dried. Then put it in your little furnace of tiles and iron hoops and melt out the wax with such heat as may be needful. Of course your wax must have been free from all impurities or it would never melt out properly. And when you have melted it out you make the fire stronger till your mould is regularly burnt, & the more it is baked the better your work will be. Then let it cool, and because the silver adapts itself more readily to the cold than to the hot mould—cold, mark you, but not moist—when it is well molten pour it in. But ere you do this, in order that it may not burn, strew a little borax over it and upon that a handful of well ground tartar [tartrate of potash], and you will find this help your work wonderfully. Then dip the mould in water in order better to separate it from the silver, and so break it open. This done, clean the silver off at the points where the channel & the vent holes come, and give it a subtle finish with the file. After this, in order to give the seal its final touches . . .

But here Cellini's directions no longer apply. Preparing a seal for a sixteenth-century Florentine cardinal involves many little refinements, such as *repoussé* work, miniature modeling, and the depiction of the cardinal's coat of arms, that are not necessary to the mass production of gold scarf pins for today's Lord and Taylor customers. Though, mark you (as Cellini would say), the scarf pins are very pretty indeed.

I found at least one other point of similarity between the *Handbook* and Cellini's accounts of his work. Goldsmiths sometimes "pickle" the metal, often annealing it or, as Staton Abbey puts it, boiling it in nitric, sulfuric, hydrochloric, or even chromic acid, in dilute solution. This is done after annealing and during various coloring processes. It brightens the metal by washing off various oxides that otherwise might have a tarnishing effect. The *Handbook* gives very careful directions as to the amounts of acid that should be used, along with other ingredients of the acid bath. Cellini's method was simpler. Get young boys, he said, and let them urinate on the piece of work. Such urine, being just acid enough, has a very cleansing effect.

I looked in vain for this suggestion in the *Handbook,* but my friend Nathan Levy, a modern-day goldsmith, knew it well. He nodded when I mentioned it.

"Oh, sure," he said. "A lot of artists believed in the purity of boys' urine. There's something about it in the accounts of Leonardo da Vinci; I think they all thought of it as something extra-special pure."

He put on the black spectacles he used for work and turned back to his bench. Nathan's studio is a small room in his apartment, and he was busy that day on a filigree job. I had asked him about the drawplate and other tools of the kind, and he showed me a braid of wire, dark brown like copper, which he said was gold.

"It's oxidized, that's all," he said. "I can clean it up in no time, but I'm making these things just now."

With tweezers and a bending tool of some sort he twisted a piece of wire into a very small curlicue, made another one like it but facing the other way, and put them together on a small metal plate. Then he dabbed liquid on them and, with a flame that never stopped burning, fused them together. The liquid, he explained, was solder, and one had to be careful not to use too much, as it would then make a big hard drop on the jewel. He picked up a ring, or at least the beginning of a ring, made of two pieces of braided wire in circlets about three quarters of an inch apart, and with great delicacy fitted the fused curlicues between them. Then he went back to making more of the filling design.

It was quiet in the workroom except for the frequent irruptions of his little boy, David, who divided his time between outdoors and in. Once when he ran outside Nathan stopped work to pick up a few objects and hand them to me.

"David made these," he said with reasonably obvious pride. "He goes to a class in this work once a week in the evening."

They were specimens of enamel, well-made and pretty.

"How old is David?" I asked.

"Eight. He's very bright, and that's a problem in a way; he's way ahead of his age in most subjects, so he's in a class of children much older and bigger than he is. The only thing he doesn't excel in is math. But when the teacher said she was worried because he's only at the ten-year level in that, I laughed. I said, 'Oh, he's only two years ahead in math? Well, I'm not going to start worrying just yet.' " He put his glasses back on and resumed work on the ring. Another piece of the pattern was fitted between the circlets.

"Nathan, who taught you how to do all this?"

He looked surprised. "Why, my father, of course. And his father taught *him,* in Yemen."

Carefully he applied more solder.

13

RELIC

No flat statement, including the one I am about to make, applies to every type of currency or currency system. Our way of using money just grew. It began with barter, as I have said, and barter has had an effect on our words for money and finance generally. For example take the word *pecuniary*. "In Germanic society," wrote Pierre Vilar in *A History of Gold and Money, 1450–1920*, "the word 'Vieh' meant both 'cattle' and 'wealth', in the same way as 'pecunia' (money) derives from 'pecus' (cattle). This was because the standard of value (the point of reference for other products) was for a long time the head of cattle (cows, oxen, etc.). Some primitive coins are stamped with an ox's head, to denote this role."

Reading this, I suddenly recalled that when the Republic of Zaire was still the Belgian Congo, the natives had one of those wise old saws that stick in the mind. "Woman," they would say oracularly, "is wealth. And wealth is woman." It was true, too—in the Belgian Congo, and in the Kingwana language. I don't know what they say there nowadays.

At any rate cows used to be units of currency for a time, and for that matter still are in some parts of Africa, where the so-called bride price might well include an agreed number of the animals, as well as spears and other valuables. But it could never have been easy, trading with cows. I try to resist the mental picture of a would-be customer going to market with a cow draped around his shoulders instead of a hundred dollars in his pocket. Ridiculous, of course, but it keeps getting in my way. I have always felt sympathy for Jack the Giant-Killer, who, you will

159

remember, swapped his mother's cow for a handful of beans. Who can blame him? Beans were much easier to carry home. He got into trouble for that; yet, if you come to think of it, he made a very good bargain. Didn't he steal the goose that laid the golden eggs from the ogre who lived at the top of the beanstalk?

When people got tired of carrying the actual object of value to market they invented a system of symbols that did just as well as cattle. But gold is no mere symbol. It had its own intrinsic worth. As we have seen, the first gold coin was minted in Lydia, and the world of Eurasia took to using golden money thereafter—those people, that is to say, who could afford it. There wasn't enough gold for everybody's coinage. But even then gold did not have to be cast in the form of coinage to be valuable as an article of trade. While it does not necessarily mean money, it does mean treasure.

Money in notes and non-gold coin is one thing, gold quite another. Money is not so tied up with emotion as is gold. Our love for gold is not rational, but consciousness of this fact does not dispel the love. We feel it. It's there. Freud, in his lecture "Anxiety and Instinctual Life," expounds a theory in keeping with his general philosophy: Gold is the same thing in human estimation, he says, as faeces. Faeces were the first gift that an infant could make, something he could part with out of love for whoever was tending him.

After this, corresponding exactly to analogous changes of meaning that occur in linguistic developments, this ancient interest in faeces is transformed into the high valuation of *gold* and *money* but also makes a contribution to the effective catharsis of *baby* and *penis.* . . . Faeces-money-gift-baby-penis are treated there [that is, in human fantasies] as though they meant the same thing, and they are represented too by the same symbols.

Well, perhaps, but I am not sure about those Freudian symbols. I once knew a Freudian who went to central Africa to study the psyche of the native but could get nowhere because, as he said in despair, the natives didn't know what he was talking about and he could not interpret their dreams. They had never seen a windmill, nor did they dream of white doves. They just didn't know what these things were. Perhaps we should simply accept the fact that we, Africans included, are fascinated by gold, and let it go at that.

Some economists, of course, won't let it go at that; our fascination is irrational and they simply won't accept it. They are too clear-headed, and that is where they go wrong. Clarity does not settle everything in our world. It was that admirably clear writer John Maynard Keynes who attacked gold in its role as unit of exchange and tried to get rid of it. In *A Tract on Monetary Reform* he wrote the statement that is invariably quoted when the subject of gold comes up, as it so often does. Gold, he said, is "a barbarous relic." He wrote his tract in 1923, when England, like the United States and many other countries, was still on the gold standard. Time has tested his dictum and found it wanting: Gold is definitely *not* a relic. At the present moment, a good long time afterward, we are not yet civilized enough to dispense with our barbarous relic. On the contrary. Yesterday in London (I write in April 1980) gold was selling at more than five hundred dollars an ounce.

In the old days when American bank notes were backed with gold, the situation was beautifully simple. On every note was a legend telling the holder in effect that the note could be redeemed in gold if one really wanted it. Naturally, in that case, most people didn't bother about doing it, which was the whole idea of holding paper money—an earnest that you could always have the gold in hand if you wished to carry around such a load. In essence the same quality held for British bank notes, and French, and so on. For those skeptics who still might doubt the United States's ability to make good its bank-note promises and pay up, there was Fort Knox to prove it: Fort Knox, which was expressly adapted to keep our gold safe. It wasn't always like that. Until 1932 government gold was held in various bank vaults here and there in the country, but the amount grew and grew until it was decided to do something really effective about security. The fort is an army reservation about thirty-five miles from Louisville, Kentucky. Originally named Camp Knox, it was founded in 1917 as a training school for the army's field artillery officers. There was a lot of room there—110,000 acres. In 1932 Camp Knox became Fort Knox. A year later the first cavalry regiment was moved in from Marfa, Texas, and was mechanized. Fort Knox was made headquarters of the armored forces in 1940, and four years later became the center of all U.S. armored troops, but before that, in 1936, the government bullion depository was constructed on its grounds, or, rather, underground. By the middle of this century the gold stocks of Fort Knox were valued (I get my information from the *Encyclopedia Britannica*) at more than $10 billion.

"The fabulous treasure," said the *Encyclopedia* writer,

is housed in a solid square bombproof building, constructed of granite, steel and concrete, enclosing a two-level torch-proof steel and concrete vault. Added security is provided by guards, sentries and an encircling steel fence, as well as by mechanical protective devices, such as the photoelectric eye. The nearby army post gives further protection.

During World War II the gold vault was used as a repository for the original copy of the U.S. Constitution and the Declaration of Independence, the Magna Carta, a copy of the Gutenberg Bible and the original draft of Lincoln's Gettysburg address.

So there it was, an enormous fortune safely locked up, at an official value of $35 an ounce. There were occasional small variations on this figure, but not enough to unbalance investors in the U.S. market. If you had money in notes, the government owed you that much in gold. Henry Mark Holzer, teacher of constitutional law, in the *Wall Street Journal* for March 17, 1975, summed up the situation:

Once upon a time, in the days before F.D.R., many types of contracts —loan agreements, bonds, mortgages—contained clauses that provided that when payment of principal, interest or both came due, it would be paid not in paper money but rather in some form of gold or in an amount of currency measured by a fixed amount of gold. The Baltimore & Ohio Railroad Co., for example, promised that for each of its $1,000 30-year 4½% bonds, issued on Feb. 1, 1930, payment of principal and interest would "be made . . . in gold coin of the United States of America of or equal to the standard of weight and fineness existing on Feb. 1, 1930."

This was no mere whim on the part of buyers and sellers, said Dr. Holzer. They knew history; they knew that to finance the Civil War the government had had to suspend gold convertability and issue "a veritable torrent of paper money." The swollen flood of currency started a landslide inflation rate of 24 percent in 1862, and within two years the dollar was worth only a third of its former value against gold. To make matters worse, the Supreme Court supported the government in its continuing issuance of paper money. That was why the Gold Clause, early in this century, became a routine provision in sales and debt contracts, "including those where the government itself was the debtor." This state of affairs persisted until 1933, when F.D.R. declared a moratorium on all banking for several days. By the time the banks opened again, the Gold Clause no longer figured in contracts, the government promise to pay gold on demand didn't hold water, and private citizens could not own gold coins, bullion, or gold certificates, because Congress had made a joint resolution to this effect. Then F.D.R. devalued the dollar 40 percent against gold. People who lost out on this action protested, and one man went to the Supreme Court about it with a test case involving the paltry sum of $38.10. He lost: The Court found for the government, holding that the Constitution declared that "the Congress shall have power . . . to coin money, regulate the value thereof, and of foreign coin. . . ." Dr. Holzer, for one, thinks that this passage does not give Congress the legal power to forbid Gold Clauses between individuals.

At any rate, once the step had been taken, more discipline became necessary. After the Second World War and, later, during the Vietnam War, the gold at Fort Knox began slipping away once more at an alarming rate. Prices were going up at home and abroad, and at our fixed value of $35 an ounce, American gold was a bargain none of the other nations ignored. People as well as nations bought and bought our gold. Watching the outflow, American economists decided that it must stop, and it was stopped abruptly. No more gold was sold from Fort Knox. Only now, since January 1976, are private citizens of the United States allowed to hold on to gold. Nowadays, suddenly, the quality magazines are full of advertisements of gold bars and coins. Dr. Holzer's voice, once sounding alone in the wilderness, is now only one among many clamoring for a reinstitution of the Gold Clause in individual contracts.

No answers can settle this complicated question forever, but one thing is certain: The lack of rationality in the human reaction to gold continues to baffle and exasperate logical people. In 1961 the economist Robert Triffin of Yale had another try at making us see reason. In *Gold and the Dollar Crisis* he wrote:

It would seem paradoxical and ludicrous to claim that the most rational economic system of international settlements conceivable in this second half of the twentieth century consists in digging holes, at immense cost, in distant corners of the world for the sole purpose of extracting gold from them, transporting it across the oceans and reburying it immediately afterward in other deep holes especially excavated to receive it and heavily guarded to protect it.

Put that way, it does indeed seem ludicrous, and Professor Triffin was not satisfied with merely saying so. At Bretton Woods he proposed a plan, a monetary unit to be accepted by all nations, that would help the world to supplant gold as a medium of exchange: He called it *bancor.* It was a good idea. The only trouble with it was that nobody would accept it. Bancor didn't get anywhere. When it came to the crunch, nations, like the people who constitute them, trusted only gold, and they pigheadedly go on trusting it. They don't trust each other's governments, or even their own, nearly as much. The minute there seems to be trouble among the higher-ups, people rush to change whatever valuables they may have into gold. Some people, like the inhabitants of India, have always collected gold, war or no war. Out of this trust in the metal, however irritating it may be to economists, has grown a financial system so huge and complicated that few individuals understand it in its entirety, but they do understand the actual heavy essence of the metal itself.

You may wonder why we get a daily quotation of gold values from London rather than some other capital, as for instance our own. It is because the system started that way and has never changed entirely, though there have been important alterations in some of the details. Investors are creatures of habit. The powerful group of gold dealers in London consists of five firms, all with long and honorable histories in the City. The oldest is Mocatta and Goldsmid, founded in 1684, which is now owned by the Standard & Banking Corporation and Dr. Henry Jarecki of New York. It is still, however, managed by a Mocatta. Second in line is Sharps, Pixley & Co., under the aegis of Kleinwort, Benson, Lonsdale Ltd.; strictly speaking, this is a combination of firms, one of which was born in 1740 and the other in 1852. They merged comparatively recently, in 1957. Third comes N. M.

Rothschild & Sons Ltd., established in 1804. Fourth is Johnson Matthey & Co. Ltd., founded in 1817. Fifth comes the baby, Samuel Montagu & Co. Ltd., born 1853. Every day these five firms, or, rather, their representatives, get together and "fix" the rate for the day, which is quoted all over the world. The meeting takes place twice during the day, in the morning and the afternoon.

The system was instituted nearly a hundred years ago, when London handled the largest amount of gold importation because South Africa shipped the output of her gold mines in the Rand, the greatest supply of gold coming in from the non-Soviet world, to London. This arrangement was broken off in 1968 for political reasons, but the influence of the old custom remained in the world of money.

"Most Wednesdays a Union Castle liner left Durban with her strongroom stacked with gold bars," wrote Timothy Green in *The World of Gold Today;* "on arrival in Southampton the bullion was swiftly transferred to the vaults of the Bank of England, which acted as selling agent for the Reserve Bank of South Africa. Since South Africa produces over 75 percent of the non-communist world's gold the London market, having cornered this gold market, was inevitably supreme." This supremacy attracted other gold-selling nations such as Rhodesia, Ghana, the Philippines, and, yes, Russia, until 1968, when the monopoly came to an end. The gold crisis shut the market for a fortnight, during which time the two-tier market was established. More about this later.

South Africa waited nearly two years before resuming full-scale gold mining. She didn't have to sell any of her stored-up gold during that time because she had a vast surplus, so the ships' loads on the Union Castle lines were comparatively small, sinking from a yearly thousand tons more or less to a mere four hundred for the whole two-year term. Even at the end of it, when shipments were resumed, South Africa began sending most of her gold to Zurich, Switzerland, and by air freight; the South Africans were angry at Britain's Labour Government for stopping arms sales to them. But the Tories came back into power in 1970, and friendly relations were re-established. There was, however, a difference now in market arrangements. To be sure, gold was again shipped in the old way, from Durban to the London vaults via Union Castle ships; it was more convenient and cheaper than air freight, and the vaults were there, the ships' strongrooms were there, and so forth. But England no longer acted as South Africa's agent in selling the gold. She merely provided house room, and her sales of gold through London traders sank to only 20 percent of the incoming metal instead of the lion's share they had previously amounted to. The rest is handled by three Swiss banks. Even so, London is outstandingly important in the gold market.

Timothy Green, who was permitted to inspect the vaults in action, gives a vivid description of what goes on there. One thing that does not go on, of course, is constant viewing by tourists; the security is formidable. But we have his word picture of the busy goblins down below the floors of the gold firms, blue-overalled men weighing gold bars, packing them into wood-fiber boxes, and sealing them for transport to the airport and the many, many countries that have bought the gold. Once one has got into the place,

one can see highly polished Russian gold, clearly emblazoned with the hammer and sickle, stacked side by side with oblong bars from the Rand Refinery in South Africa or squat, square American bars stamped by the U.S. Assay Office. Each bar must be up to the exacting "good-delivery" standards of the London market by being at least 995 parts per thousand pure gold, containing between 350 and 430 troy ounces of fine gold and bearing a serial number and stamp of one of the forty-nine firms in fourteen countries who are approved as melters and assayers.

The blue-clad men are muscular. They have to be, to handle four-hundred-ounce bars, but not all the gold in the vaults is in such heavy form. There are ten-tola bars for India (ten tolas are 3.75 ounces), which are a popular size for smugglers. Malaysia prefers ten-ounce bars, and there is a brisk sale of kilo bars to Switzerland, France, Beirut, and Kuwait.

The representatives of the five dealers who fix the daily price of gold for the world's stock markets meet every working day at the Rothschild offices in St. Swithin's Lane at 10:30 A.M. and 3:30 P.M. The ceremony dates back to September 12, 1919, and is the result of a determination on the part of the firms to simplify matters for the unfortunate Rothschild bullion broker who until then had had to visit all the other offices in person to offer South African gold and see what they would pay. Then some bright soul suggested using the telephone, and things were much easier. According to Green, the gold-fixing room is spacious, with an olive green carpet, green chairs, and portraits on the walls of the many European monarchs for whom the Rothschilds used to negotiate loans. The manager of the firm's bullion and foreign exchange department sits at the end of the long table in the center of the room, a calculating machine in front of him. The four visitors, sitting along the walls, each have a desk furnished with a telephone (with an open line to his own firm's trading room) and a little supine British flag, the Union Jack. He uses the flag to stop the meeting whenever he wishes to consult his trading room: He stands it up, and to the cry of "Flag up!" the others obediently suspend operations while he confers on the telephone. At the other end of the line, of course, is a man who is in contact with clients all over the place, in Europe or New York. When he has received instructions, he lowers his flag and everyone goes on with his business.

But before this happens, of course, trading must begin. The Rothschild man says, "Gentlemen, we will start at four hundred and forty," or whatever has been decided, depending on what the sum was at the close of yesterday's operations plus any recent developments in the state of the world. (Incidentally the price is in dollars. Why? Because that is the way it's done.) The dealers then speak up if they are selling or buying for their clients. Sometimes no seller speaks up at the opening, and then the price is moved up ten cents the first time, then five cents, until somebody breaks the silence by offering gold. A similar rite is followed for buyers, but then of course the price is reduced, ten cents at first, then five cents a time. When the silence has been broken by both sellers and buyers, the Rothschild agent says, "Figures, please," and the others give them: Mocatta so many bars, Sharps so many, and so forth, each in turn. If there is enough gold to meet the buyers' demand, the price is then fixed.

"There is, of course, no compulsion for a member of the market to do all, or indeed any, of his business at fixing," says Green. He can "marry up" his own buying and selling orders outside. Much actual buying and selling is done after the fixing is over, throughout the day, with the price fluctuating. But the Bank of England found the daily figure very useful and kept an open telephone line to Rothschild's trading room when it was agent for all South Africa's gold production. After all, the bank was buying for the international gold pool. This was easy enough in the old days when the United States kept her official price in the neighborhood of $35. If it went over $32.20, the Bank of England sold off enough to keep it down, and all was peaceful if not very interesting. Then came the Second World War, and the London gold market was suspended until March 1954. Nothing much happened—nothing unusual, that is to say—until October 1960, just before the American presidential election. Speculation ran wild as to whether the new president would devalue the dollar, and the gold price shot up to over $40. The Bank of England sold gold and brought it down, but this turned out to be only a temporary expedient. Time and time again the bank, with the agreement of other members of the pool, shoved the price of gold back within the sacred limits, until there came a time—November 1967— when England herself devalued sterling. After that it was a scramble, and the magic figure of $35 (or thereabouts), often endangered, looked doomed when the Vietnam War dragged on and on. It became the fashion, of course, to buy gold, and the demand reached unprecedented heights.

"What the pool had not reckoned with," wrote Green, ". . . was the extent to which countless speculators who had never even thought of buying gold before suddenly found it the fashionable gamble that week. Men who usually stuck sternly to cocoa or coffee futures got the word from their brokers that this was just not cocoa's week. Try gold instead."

March 14, 1968, was a Thursday. That afternoon when the London market closed it was clear that something had to be done to stem the gold rush, and it was decided to close the market. Accordingly, Friday, March 15, was declared a bank holiday, which was prolonged for two weeks. During this time the chief bankers met in Washington and came to an agreement which was quickly announced: The gold pool was ended, and from then on there would be a two-tier price system, which meant that central banks would continue to deal with each other on the basis of $35 an ounce for gold, but there would be a free market price for everybody else, at which gold could find its own level. For two years everything went well, which is to say that after a preliminary flurry, when the London price did go up to $40 and more, it went back to about $35. This had the effect of pushing the speculators out. But by the end of 1971 it was on its way up again, to nearly $40. At the beginning of May 1972 it passed the $50 mark; by June it was in the $60s, in August it reached $70—and when the United States devalued in February 1973, it shot up past $90. According to Green, "Montagu's *Annual Bullion Review* even forecast $100 price soon."

His book was published in 1973, and that prophecy failed to shock. I am writing this chapter in April 1980. On April 19 the gold price in London was reported as $512.50.

Just what hit the world nobody is quite sure, but all of a sudden everyone was buying or selling gold. We had never seen such a rush on such a scale. It seemed to happen all over the place, and records came tumbling in across the financial telephone lines, from London, Paris, Milan, California, South America, wherever you can think of except behind the Iron Curtain, where God knows what was going on. People sold, people bought, not merely stocks, shares, bonds, and other forms of paper, but the metal itself, the hard yellow stuff. The gold rate went up and up until it hovered in the neighborhood of 800, which means eight hundred dollars per ounce. Then it approached 900. On 47th Street in Manhattan, the city's gold-trading center, there was talk of gold's breaking through the 1000 mark, but it hesitated in its climb before hitting that pinnacle, turned, and wobbled. It didn't crash, but just seesawed between 630 and the upper reaches, like the craziest thermometer in the world.

Of course, to have a gold market you must have lots of people like you and me, the owners. Well, you had them, quite a lot of them. One by one these owners became aware of what was going on from reading newspaper stories and advertisements. They discovered that people were gathering up their old pieces of broken gold (and silver as well; silver rode along on gold's coat-tails) and trotting out to sell them for the best possible price. The papers were full of notices, saying, Selling Your Gold? We Give Highest Prices. Some of us still lingered timidly in front of the TV set, but there we saw long lines of ordinary people like ourselves, waiting to have their gold and/or silver appraised and bought if the price was right. Overnight we grew technical. Shabby old brooches suddenly looked like hitherto unsuspected wealth, as well as discarded tooth fillings which for years had lain in an old plastic tumbler in a corner of the medicine cabinet. The necklace bequeathed by Aunt Mary as a family heirloom: Was it really gold or just pinchbeck? And the Revere bowl: "Darling," we asked, "would you just turn it over and see if there's a hallmark on the bottom? We never use it."

"I had two little pieces of gold chain," said Andrea, who works in an office. "They were just scraps, and I wasn't even sure if they were real gold. One was off a bracelet, the other from a broken necklace, and both had been out of style for years. I wondered if it was any use giving my lunch hour to selling them, or if I could, even. People would probably think I was a total maniac, I thought. Anyway I put them into my pocket and went along to one of the places advertising on Forty-seventh Street, though I told myself those miserable little chains couldn't be more than ten dollars' worth. I'd read an article that morning on comparison-shopping between gold dealers and buyers. One of the advertisers was a smelter I found in the Yellow Pages, so I went there. A crowd had already gathered outside the door, and there was a guard who looked at me and said, 'You. You there. You have to get in line outside.' So I meekly went outside and lined up with a lot of women who were all wearing fur coats and obviously had jewelry to spare. They were talking among themselves about the best place for selling, evidently the Empire State Building, only there you had to start waiting at seven thirty in the morning. I felt silly with my tiny chains.

"Then a dark, good-looking man came along and shouted to all of us, 'How much per pennyweight?' I didn't know what he meant, but one of the women yelled back, 'Thirteen,' and he said, "I'll give you seventeen. Come with me."

"I didn't go with him, though some of the others did. I don't know why, exactly. I just didn't trust him. I waited about another hour at that place, but they were awfully slow, one man taking care of everybody. There were about five lines, so finally I walked away and went on to another place nearby where they were buying gold."

She never did find anyone to explain the pennyweight system, but she sold her two little chains, having turned down one offer of thirty dollars, for an even fifty dollars. It was a delightful surprise.

"To tell you the truth," she admitted, "I got so much into the spirit of things that I thought of selling this." She pointed to a gold ring she was wearing. "Then I thought, why should I sell it? I *like* it, and I've got fifty dollars I never expected. I'm glad I didn't sell the ring. It's a funny feeling, selling gold. You'd think I would have felt richer after getting that fifty dollars, but I didn't; I felt poor. There's a man in our office who had a gold fountain pen that he never used, and he sold that and got a really big price . . . but I felt poor, and I don't know why."

Obviously, as individuals we don't live forever. Even as a species we won't endure that long. But one thing seems certain: As long as the human race endures, one of its characteristics will not die out—its love of and trust in gold. I doubt if it will disappear until the last human being stops breathing.

SELECTED BIBLIOGRAPHY

Abbey, Staton. *The Goldsmith's and Silversmith's Handbook.* New York: D. Van Nostrand Company, 1952.

Allen, Gina. *Gold!* New York: Thomas Y. Crowell Company, 1964.

Boxer, C. R. "Brazilian Gold and British Traders in the First Half of the Eighteenth Century," *The Hispanic American Historical Review,* vol. xlix, no. 3 (August 1969), pp. 454–72.

———. *The Golden Age of Brazil, 1695–1750: Growing Pains of a Colonial Society.* Berkeley, Cal.: University of California Press, 1962.

Cellini, Benvenuto. *The Treatises of Benvenuto Cellini on Goldsmithing and Sculpture.* Translated by C. R. Ashbee. New York: Dover Publications, 1967.

Einzig, Paul. *Primitive Money in Its Ethnological, Historical, and Economic Aspects,* 2nd ed. New York: Pergamon Press, 1966.

Green, Timothy. *The World of Gold Today,* rev. ed. New York: Walker & Company, 1973.

Hinckle, Warren, 3rd, and Frederic Hobbs, eds. *The Richest Place on Earth: The Story of Virginia City, Nevada, and the Heyday of the Comstock Lode.* Boston: Houghton Mifflin Company, 1978.

Keynes, John Maynard. *A Tract on Monetary Reform.* London: Macmillan & Co., 1924.

Story, Mickey. *Centrifugal Casting as a Jewelry Process.* Scranton, Pa.: International Textbook Company, 1963.

Triffin, Robert. *Gold and the Dollar Crisis: The Future of Convertibility.* New Haven, Conn.: Yale University Press, 1961.

Vilar, Pierre. *A History of Gold and Money, 1450–1920.* Translated by Judith White. Atlantic Highlands, N.J.: Humanities Press, 1976.

Wagner, Kip, and L. B. Taylor, Jr. *Pieces of Eight: Recovering the Riches of a Lost Spanish Treasure Fleet.* New York: E. P. Dutton & Co., 1966.

INDEX